Southern Living®

ALL-TIME FAVORITE

CHICKEN
RECIPES

Southern Living®

ALL-TIME FAVORITE

CHICKEN RECIPES

Compiled and Edited by
Jean Wickstrom Liles

Oxmoor House®

Copyright 1995 by Oxmoor House, Inc.
Book Division of Southern Progress Corporation
P.O. Box 2465, Birmingham, Alabama 35201

Library of Congress Catalog Number: 95-67711
ISBN: 0-8487-2220-5
Manufactured in the United States of America
First Printing 1995

Editor-in-Chief: Nancy J. Fitzpatrick
Editorial Director, Special Interest Publications: Ann H. Harvey
Senior Foods Editor: Susan Carlisle Payne
Senior Editor, Editorial Services: Olivia Kindig Wells
Art Director: James Boone

Southern Living ® ALL-TIME FAVORITE CHICKEN RECIPES

Menu and Recipe Consultant: Jean Wickstrom Liles
Assistant Editor: Kelly Hooper Troiano
Copy Editor: Jane Phares
Editorial Assistant: Keri Bradford
Indexer: Mary Ann Laurens
Concept Designer: Melissa Jones Clark
Designer: Rita Yerby
Senior Photographers: Jim Bathie; Charles Walton IV, *Southern Living* magazine
Photographers: Ralph Anderson; Tina Evans, J. Savage Gibson, Sylvia Martin, *Southern Living* magazine
Senior Photo Stylist: Kay E. Clarke
Photo Stylists: Virginia R. Cravens; Leslie Byars, Ashley Johnson, *Southern Living* magazine
Production and Distribution Director: Phillip Lee
Production Manager: Gail Morris
Associate Production and Distribution Manager: John Charles Gardner
Associate Production Manager: Theresa L. Beste
Production Assistant: Marianne Jordan

Our appreciation to the editorial staff of *Southern Living* magazine for their contributions to this volume.

Cover: Quick Chicken with Rainbow Pepper Topping (recipes on page 68)
Page 1: Double-Crust Chicken Pot Pie (recipe on page 48)
Page 2: Italian Chicken Cutlets (recipe on page 102) and Asparagus-Chicken Salad (recipe on page 30)

Contents

Chicken—A Perfect Choice   6

Appetizers and Snacks   11

Salad Sampler   23

Comfort Food   39

Roasted and Baked   53

Versatile Chicken Breasts   67

Chicken Combos   85

From the Skillet and Wok   99

South by Southwest   113

Outdoor Specialties   127

Chicken—A Perfect Choice

You can always count on chicken to be a favorite with family and guests.
Its popularity is due in part to the endless variety of dishes it creates:
dinner entrées, luncheon specialties, or tempting appetizers.
Thanks to its delicate flavor, chicken teams well with fruits and
vegetables and takes naturally to many seasonings and cooking methods.

Chicken—What's Available

At the supermarket, chicken is available in a variety of cuts and products. You'll find packages of whole chicken, chicken halves or quarters, cut-up parts, breast halves, boned breasts, thighs, drumsticks, and wings, plus a variety of semi-prepared and fully cooked products. Select the cut that best suits your time and budget requirements. Keep in mind that the less processed the chicken, the less expensive it will be per pound.

• **Whole broiler-fryer**: This all-purpose chicken is usually the least expensive per pound and weighs 3 to 4½ pounds. It's suitable not only for broiling and frying, but also for roasting, baking, and grilling, and is packaged with and without neck and giblets.

• **Young roaster**: Also known as a roasting chicken, this large, meaty chicken ranges from 5 to 8 pounds and provides more meat per pound than smaller chickens.

• **Cut-up chicken**: Usually a whole broiler-fryer cut into 8 pieces, this package yields 2 breast halves and 2 each of thighs, drumsticks, and wings.

• **Broiler halves or splits**: A broiler is cut into 2 pieces of approximately equal weight and is ideal for grilling.

• **Broiler quarters**: Leg quarters and breast quarters are usually packaged separately. A leg quarter, which is all dark meat, includes a drumstick, thigh, and back portion. A breast quarter, which is all white meat, includes a wing, breast, and back portion.

• **Leg**: The whole leg is all dark meat with unseparated drumstick and thigh.

• **Drumstick**: This is the lower portion of the leg. Allow 2 drumsticks per adult serving.

• **Thigh**: This meaty portion above the knee joint is a favorite of those who prefer dark meat. Thighs are also available skinned and boned and can usually be substituted for skinned and boned chicken breast halves. Allow 1 or 2 thighs per person, depending on the special dish size. See the recipe for Soy-Lime Grilled Chicken Thighs on page 131.

- **Breast halves or split breast**: Popular because of their tender, meaty character, breasts are all white meat. They can be purchased whole or split, bone-in or boned, and skin-on or skinned.
- **Wing**: The whole wing has 3 sections attached and is all white meat.
- **Drummette**: This first section of the wing makes ideal hors d'oeuvres.
- **Giblets**: The gizzard, liver, and heart are 100 percent edible, and when simmered for a few hours, add flavor to your chicken broth.
- **Ground chicken**: Popular as a low-fat replacement for ground beef or pork, ground chicken is made from skinned and boned thigh meat.
- **Other packaged products**: A wide selection of prepared and semi-prepared products are available frozen and fresh in your local supermarket. Partially prepared products include chicken pieces that have been marinated or seasoned but haven't been cooked. Some of the fully cooked products include roasters and whole broilers that are ready to eat.

Tips on Buying and Storing Chicken

- Check for the USDA Grade A inspection mark on a label to insure the chicken meets highest government standards for safety and wholesomeness.
- Check the "sell by" date on package label indicating the last day the products should be sold. Chicken will retain its freshness for a few days after this date if properly refrigerated.
- A chicken's skin color ranges from white to deep yellow, depending on the chicken's diet. Color doesn't indicate a difference in nutritional value, flavor, fat content, or tenderness. Color of giblets also varies and doesn't indicate a taste difference.
- Refrigerate raw chicken promptly after you

purchase it. Never leave chicken on a countertop at room temperature.
- Tray-packed raw chicken can be safely stored in its original wrap for up to 2 days in the coldest part of the refrigerator. Freeze raw chicken if it is not to be used within 2 days.
- Never let cooked chicken stand at room temperature for more than 2 hours. If not eaten immediately, cooked chicken should be kept either hot (between 140° and 165°) or refrigerated at 40° or less. Store cooked chicken for picnics in an ice chest or insulated container.
- Cooked chicken, properly wrapped and refrigerated, should be used within 2 days.
- If cooked chicken is stuffed, remove stuffing and refrigerate chicken and stuffing in separate containers.

Handle Chicken with Care

Chicken, like all fresh meat, is very perishable and must be handled with care to maintain top quality. Use these tips when handling and preparing chicken:

- Wash hands thoroughly with hot soapy water before and after handling raw poultry.
- Cut raw poultry on acrylic or hard plastic cutting boards rather than wooden or porous surfaces that are hard to clean thoroughly.
- Clean countertops, cutting surfaces, and utensils with hot soapy water after handling raw chicken in order to prevent spreading bacteria to other foods.
- Rinse chicken and pat dry with paper towels before cooking.
- Marinate chicken in the refrigerator. When grilling chicken, do not place cooked chicken on the same plate used to transport raw chicken to the grill without washing the plate.
- If leftovers need to be reheated, cover to retain moisture and to insure that chicken heats all the way through.

Freezing and Thawing Guide

Chicken is very perishable and should be cooked within 2 days of purchasing. If it is not cooked within that time, follow these tips for freezing and thawing:

• Remove raw chicken from original package; wash and pat dry. For best results, wrap chicken pieces individually or in portions to suit your family size. Wrap tightly in heavy-duty plastic wrap, aluminum foil, or freezer paper; store in a large plastic freezer bag. To prevent freezer burn, press air out of bag before sealing. Label package with date and contents.

• Prepare cooked chicken for freezing as indicated above. If chicken is cooked in a sauce, gravy, or other liquid, pack it in a sturdy freezer container with a tight-fitting lid.

• Do not freeze a stuffed chicken for later roasting. Always stuff chicken just before cooking.

• Thaw chicken that is well wrapped in the refrigerator—never at room temperature. Allow 24 hours to thaw a 4-pound whole chicken in the refrigerator and 3 to 9 hours for chicken parts, depending on the weight of the chicken.

• To thaw chicken safely in cold water, place chicken in a watertight plastic bag and submerge in cold water; change water frequently. It takes about 2 hours to thaw a whole chicken.

• Use the microwave for quick thawing of chicken (cooked or uncooked). Defrosting time varies according to whether chicken is whole or if parts are frozen together. Remove the chicken from the freezer wrapping, place in a microwave-safe dish, and cover. Microwave at DEFROST or MEDIUM-LOW (30% power) 2 minutes. Let stand 2 minutes. Separate chicken parts as they begin to thaw, and rotate chicken to prevent overcooking of certain parts. Repeat if necessary.

• Cooked or uncooked chicken that has been thawed should not be refrozen. Cook the thawed chicken immediately or refrigerate it until cooking time.

Guidelines for Chicken Cookery

Whatever your choice of cooking method, always cook chicken well-done, not medium or rare. Follow these suggestions for cooking chicken safely:

• A meat thermometer provides the most accurate doneness test for cooking chicken. For a whole chicken, a meat thermometer inserted into the thickest part of the thigh (not touching bone or fat) should register 180°. The legs should move freely when twisted. Bone-in parts should reach an internal temperature of 170° and boneless parts should reach 160°.

• Without the use of a thermometer, check visually for doneness by piercing chicken with a fork or cutting chicken with a knife. The juices should run clear, and the chicken should no longer look pink.

• When microwaving chicken, it is better to undercook than overcook because it can be returned to the microwave for additional cooking if it isn't done.

• Do not partially cook chicken and store it to be finished later, as this delay can promote the growth of bacteria.

For Quick Chopped Cooked Chicken

Many recipes call for tender chunks of chopped cooked chicken. To cook, follow directions on page 9 for Simmering or Microwaving.

• 1 pound skinned and boned breast or thigh meat yields about 2 cups chopped cooked chicken. A single chicken breast will yield about ½ cup chopped cooked chicken.

• A 3-pound broiler-fryer yields 2½ to 3 cups chopped cooked chicken.

• A 6- to 7-pound roaster yields about 7 cups chopped cooked chicken.

• Leftover chopped cooked chicken can be stored in freezer bags and frozen up to 1 month.

Basic Cooking Techniques

These basic cooking methods can be the beginning of many creative chicken dishes.

The popularity of chicken is quite understandable since it can be the basis for any number of dishes and takes well to a variety of cooking methods.

Frying

Step 1: Dredge chicken pieces in seasoned flour.

Step 2: Pour vegetable oil to depth of 1 inch in a heavy skillet; heat to medium-high temperature. Add chicken and cook, uncovered, for 10 minutes, turning to brown both sides. Reduce heat to medium-low; cover and cook 20 minutes or until chicken is tender. Drain on paper towels.

Simmering

Place broiler-fryer (whole or cut-up) or about 3 pounds of skinned chicken pieces in a Dutch oven. Add 4 cups water, 1 teaspoon salt, ¼ teaspoon pepper, 3 celery tops, and 1 onion, quartered. Cover and simmer 45 minutes or until chicken is tender. Remove chicken from Dutch oven and cool. Skin and bone chicken; cut chicken into bite-size pieces. (For boned chicken breasts, simmer 15 to 20 minutes.)

Roasting

Season whole chicken inside and out with salt and pepper. If stuffing chicken, spoon dressing loosely into cavity. Tie legs together with string, or close cavity with skewers. Hook wing tips under back of chicken. Place, breast side up, on a rack in a shallow roasting pan. Bake at 350° for 1½ hours or until internal temperature reaches 180°, basting as recipe directs. Let stand 10 minutes before carving.

Microwaving

Remove skin from chicken. Arrange chicken pieces in a shallow microwave dish in a single layer with meatier parts toward outside of dish. Brush chicken with melted butter. Cover loosely with wax paper or heavy-duty plastic wrap with corner vented. Microwave parts at HIGH and whole chicken on MEDIUM (50% power). Microwave about 6 minutes per pound, rotating or rearranging to promote even cooking. Sprinkle with salt and let stand, covered, 5 to 10 minutes.

Grilling

Place chicken halves, quarters, or pieces, skin side up, on prepared grill positioned 6 to 8 inches above heat source. Grill chicken over direct or indirect heat, turning frequently with tongs. (See page 139 for instructions.) For extra flavor and juiciness, brush chicken often with a basting sauce. Brush with a sweet sauce in last 15 minutes of grilling only to avoid overbrowning.

Preparation Techniques

These techniques and tips for preparing chicken will help you with the wide assortment of recipes in this book.

Boning a Chicken Breast

If you're in a hurry, skinned and boned chicken breast halves make cooking quick and easy. If you have time, however, you may appreciate the economy of boning the breasts at home.

Step 1: Carefully remove the skin from the chicken breast, and discard. Split the breast in half lengthwise with a sharp knife.

Step 2: Starting at the breast-bone side of the chicken, slice meat away from the bone, using a thin, sharp knife, cutting as close to the bone as possible. Remove the tendon; this prevents shrinkage and makes the meat tender for serving.

Skinning Chicken Pieces

Almost half the fat in chicken comes from the skin and the pockets of fat just under the skin. To lower the fat content even further, remove the skin and cut away any excess fat before or after cooking.

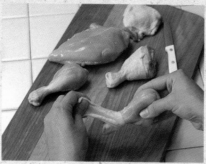

Cutting Chicken into Strips

To prepare chicken for stir-fries and other dishes calling for chicken strips, place skinned and boned chicken on a cutting surface. Cut each breast half into 3 or 4 long, thin strips (about ¾-inch wide), using a sharp knife. Then proceed as recipe directs.

Flattening a Chicken Breast

Place skinned and boned chicken breast between 2 sheets of wax paper or heavy-duty plastic wrap. Press out and down from center with a meat mallet so breast flattens evenly to desired thickness. This yields a thinner breast that rolls or stuffs easily and cooks quickly.

Marinating Chicken

Enhance the flavor of grilled, roasted, or microwaved chicken by refrigerating it in a flavorful marinade. Place chicken in a shallow dish or heavy-duty, zip-top plastic bag; add marinade and refrigerate. Drain chicken; cook as desired.

Appetizers & Snacks

When it comes to versatility in appetizers and snacks, there's no match for chicken. Enjoy drummettes, pizza, nachos, and sandwiches— all perfect for chicken nibbling.

Coconut Curried Chicken Balls, Festive Chicken Spread, Wine Pâté

Peppery Chicken in Pita, Marinated Chicken in a Sandwich, Chicken Crêpes

Chicken-Chile Cheesecake, Curried Chicken Cheesecake, Rumaki, Hot Buffalo Wings

Spicy Chicken Strips, Chicken Almondette Fingers, Chicken Nachos

Southwestern Chicken Drummettes (page 16)

Coconut Curried Chicken Balls

⅔ cup raisins
2 tablespoons dark rum
4 skinned chicken breast halves
1⅓ cups pineapple cream cheese
3 tablespoons mango chutney
3 tablespoons mayonnaise or salad dressing
1 tablespoon teriyaki sauce
2 teaspoons curry powder
½ teaspoon ground ginger
½ teaspoon salt
¼ teaspoon red pepper
1 cup sliced almonds, toasted
1½ cups flaked coconut
Garnishes: apricots, orange slices, kiwifruit

Combine raisins and rum; set aside.

Place chicken in a large saucepan; cover with water. Bring to a boil; cover, reduce heat, and simmer 25 minutes or until tender. Remove chicken; let cool slightly, and bone. Position knife blade in food processor bowl; add half of chicken. Pulse 2 or 3 times until chicken is coarsely chopped. Repeat with remaining chicken.

Combine cream cheese and next 7 ingredients. Drain raisins. Add raisins, chicken, and almonds to cream cheese mixture, stirring until blended. Shape mixture into 1-inch balls; roll in coconut. Chill before serving. Arrange on a platter, and garnish, if desired. **Yield: 44 appetizers.**

Note: These may be frozen up to 1 week.

Chicken Salad Spread

1½ cups coarsely ground cooked chicken
¼ cup sweet pickle relish
3 'to 4 tablespoons mayonnaise
2 tablespoons finely chopped onion
¾ teaspoon salt
½ teaspoon celery seeds
¼ teaspoon pepper

Combine all ingredients, stirring well. Store in refrigerator; serve with crackers. **Yield: 1½ cups.**

Festive Chicken Spread

1 (8-ounce) package cream cheese, softened
3 tablespoons mayonnaise
1 tablespoon lemon juice
½ teaspoon salt
¼ teaspoon ground ginger
⅛ teaspoon pepper
4 drops of hot sauce
2 cups diced cooked chicken
2 hard-cooked eggs, diced
¼ cup diced green onions
3 tablespoons chopped green pepper
Green pepper strips
2 tablespoons sesame seeds, toasted
3 tablespoons chopped black olives
3 tablespoons chopped sweet red pepper
5 slices cucumber, halved (optional)
Parsley sprigs (optional)

Combine first 7 ingredients in a large bowl; beat at medium speed of an electric mixer until smooth. Add chicken, eggs, green onions, and chopped green pepper; stir well.

Line a 1-quart bowl or mold with plastic wrap. Spoon mixture into bowl; press firmly with the back of a spoon. Cover and chill at least 4 hours.

Invert bowl onto serving platter. Remove bowl, and peel off plastic wrap. Garnish mound with green pepper strips, sesame seeds, black olives, and sweet red pepper. Arrange cucumber slices and parsley sprigs around bottom of mound, if desired; serve with assorted crackers. **Yield: 3 cups.**

Wine Pâté

¼ cup butter or margarine
1 pound chicken livers
½ cup sliced fresh mushrooms
⅓ cup chopped green onions
1 clove garlic, minced
¾ teaspoon salt
½ cup dry white wine
½ cup butter or margarine, softened
Pinch of dried dillweed
3 or 4 drops of hot sauce

Melt ¼ cup butter in a skillet. Add livers and next 4 ingredients; sauté 5 minutes. Add wine and remaining ingredients; cover and simmer 10 minutes. Cool slightly.

Pour mixture into container of an electric blender; blend until smooth. Pour into a lightly oiled 3-cup mold; cover and chill at least 8 hours. Unmold and serve pâté with assorted crackers. **Yield: 3 cups.**

Chicken Liver Pâté

⅓ cup finely chopped onion
2 tablespoons butter or margarine, melted
½ pound chicken livers
¼ teaspoon salt
2 tablespoons dry sherry
½ cup butter, softened

Cook onion in 2 tablespoons butter in a skillet over medium heat until tender; add chicken livers and cook 10 to 15 minutes, stirring often.

Pour livers into container of an electric blender. Add salt and sherry; process until smooth. Cool mixture.

Combine liver mixture and ½ cup butter; place in a small bowl or crock, and serve with crackers. **Yield: about 1½ cups.**

Chicken-Chile Cheesecake

1⅓ cups finely crushed tortilla chips
¼ cup butter or margarine, melted
3 (8-ounce) packages cream cheese, softened
4 large eggs
1 teaspoon chili powder
1 teaspoon Worcestershire sauce
¼ teaspoon salt
3 tablespoons minced green onions
1½ cups finely shredded cooked chicken
2 (4.5-ounce) cans chopped green chiles, drained
1½ cups (6 ounces) shredded Monterey Jack cheese
1 (16-ounce) carton sour cream
1 teaspoon seasoned salt
Garnish: minced green onions
Picante sauce

Combine tortilla chips and butter; press on bottom and 1 inch up sides of a 9-inch springform pan. Set aside.

Beat cream cheese at high speed of an electric mixer until light and fluffy; add eggs, one at a time, beating well after each addition. Stir in chili powder and next 3 ingredients.

Pour half of cream cheese mixture into prepared pan. Sprinkle with chicken, chiles, and cheese; carefully pour remaining cream cheese mixture on top.

Bake at 350° for 10 minutes; reduce heat to 300°, and bake an additional hour or until set. Cool completely on a wire rack.

Combine sour cream and seasoned salt, stirring well; spread evenly on top of cheesecake. Cover and chill at least 8 hours. Garnish, if desired, and serve with picante sauce. **Yield: 8 servings or 24 appetizer servings.**

Curried Chicken Cheesecake

Curried Chicken Cheesecake

1⅓ cups round buttery cracker crumbs
¼ cup butter or margarine, melted
1½ teaspoons chicken-flavored bouillon
    granules
1 tablespoon boiling water
3 (8-ounce) packages cream cheese, softened
3 large eggs
1 (8-ounce) carton sour cream
3 tablespoons grated onion
3 tablespoons minced celery
1 tablespoon all-purpose flour
2 to 3 teaspoons curry powder
¼ teaspoon salt
1½ cups chopped cooked chicken
½ cup chopped almonds, toasted
⅓ cup golden raisins
Lettuce leaves
Garnishes: chopped sweet red pepper, flaked
    coconut, chopped green pepper
Assorted condiments
Curried Sour Cream Sauce

Combine crumbs and butter; press on bottom
and 1 inch up sides of a 9-inch springform pan.
Set aside.

Combine bouillon granules and boiling water;
stir until granules dissolve.

Beat cream cheese at high speed of an electric
mixer until light and fluffy; add eggs, one at a
time, beating well after each addition. Add bouillon mixture, sour cream, and next 5 ingredients;
beat at low speed until blended. Stir in chicken,
almonds, and raisins.

Pour mixture into prepared pan. Bake at 300°
for 45 minutes or until set. Turn oven off, and
partially open oven door; leave cheesecake in
oven 1 hour. Remove from oven, and let cool
completely on a wire rack. Cover and chill.

Unmold cheesecake onto a lettuce-lined platter; garnish, if desired. Serve cheesecake with
several of the following condiments: flaked
coconut, toasted slivered almonds, chutney,
chopped green or sweet red pepper, raisins, and
crumbled cooked bacon. Serve with Curried Sour
Cream Sauce. **Yield: 8 servings or 24 appetizer
servings.**

Curried Sour Cream Sauce

1 (8-ounce) carton sour cream
1½ teaspoons curry powder
⅛ teaspoon ground ginger

Combine all ingredients, stirring well; cover
and chill. **Yield: 1 cup.**

Rumaki

About ½ pound chicken livers
¼ cup soy sauce
1½ tablespoons dry white wine
2 cloves garlic, minced
⅛ teaspoon ground ginger
1 (6-ounce) can water chestnuts, drained
12 slices bacon, cut into thirds

Cut chicken livers in about 1-inch pieces.
Combine soy sauce, wine, garlic, and ginger in a
shallow dish or heavy-duty zip-top plastic bag;
mix well. Add chicken livers. Cover dish or seal
bag and marinate in refrigerator 2 to 3 hours.

Cut water chestnuts in half. Place a water chest-
nut half and a piece of chicken liver on each piece
of bacon. Roll up, and secure with a wooden pick.

Arrange appetizers on paper-towel-lined
microwave-safe platters, placing no more than a
dozen appetizers on each. Cover and refrigerate
up to 2 hours.

Cover platters with paper towels when ready to
microwave. Microwave each platter at HIGH 4½ to
7 minutes or until bacon is crisp and liver is done,
giving dish one half-turn. **Yield: about 3 dozen.**

Note: Rumaki may be microwaved without
final chilling. Microwave time will be the same.

Hot Buffalo Wings

2½ pounds chicken wings
1 teaspoon salt
¼ teaspoon pepper
Vegetable oil
¼ cup hot sauce
¼ cup water
¼ cup butter or margarine
1 tablespoon cider vinegar

Cut chicken wings in half at joint; cut off tips of wings, and discard. Sprinkle chicken with salt and pepper.

Pour oil to depth of 2 inches into a large, heavy skillet; heat to 350°. Fry wings, about 1 dozen at a time, for 10 minutes. Drain on paper towels. Arrange wings in a 13- x 9- x 2-inch dish.

Combine hot sauce and remaining ingredients in a small saucepan; cook over low heat until butter melts. Pour over fried wings.

Bake, uncovered, at 350° for 10 to 15 minutes or until hot. **Yield: 3 dozen appetizers.**

Southwestern Chicken Drummettes

(pictured on page 11)

⅔ cup fine, dry breadcrumbs
⅔ cup finely crushed corn chips
1 (1¼-ounce) package taco seasoning mix
2 pounds chicken drummettes, skinned
1 (16-ounce) jar taco sauce, divided

Combine first 3 ingredients in a small bowl. Dip drummettes, one at a time, into ½ cup taco sauce, and dredge in crumb mixture; place on a lightly greased baking sheet.

Bake at 375° for 30 to 35 minutes. Serve with remaining taco sauce. **Yield: 8 to 10 appetizer servings.**

Spicy Chicken Strips

8 skinned and boned chicken breast halves
¾ cup all-purpose flour
1 to 1½ teaspoons chili powder
¾ teaspoon salt
½ teaspoon garlic powder
¼ teaspoon ground cumin
¼ teaspoon pepper
1 large egg, beaten
½ cup water
Vegetable oil
Tomato-Garlic Dip

Cut chicken into long, thin strips (about ¾-inch wide). Combine flour and next 5 ingredients; stir well. Stir in egg and water. Dip chicken strips in batter.

Fry strips, a few at a time, in hot oil (375°) for 2 to 3 minutes or until golden. Drain on paper towels. Serve immediately with Tomato-Garlic Dip. **Yield: 16 appetizer servings.**

Tomato-Garlic Dip

1 (6-ounce) can tomato paste
⅓ cup mayonnaise
¼ cup sour cream
¼ cup tomato sauce
2 cloves garlic, crushed
¼ teaspoon ground cumin
¼ teaspoon chili powder
¼ teaspoon hot sauce

Combine all ingredients in a small bowl; stir well. Serve dip in a hollowed-out cabbage bowl, if desired. **Yield: 1½ cups.**

Spicy Chicken Strips

Chicken Almondette Fingers

1 (8-ounce) package tempura batter mix
1 (12-ounce) can beer
1 cup flaked coconut
½ cup sliced almonds
6 skinned and boned chicken breast halves,
    cut into 24 strips
Vegetable oil
Honey-Poppy Seed Sauce

Combine tempura batter mix and beer; pour into a shallow dish, and set aside. Combine coconut and almonds. Dip each chicken strip into batter mixture, and dredge in coconut mixture.

Pour oil to depth of 1½ inches in a Dutch oven; heat to 350°. Fry chicken strips 2 minutes on each side or until golden; drain. Serve with Honey-Poppy Seed Sauce. **Yield: 24 appetizers.**

Honey-Poppy Seed Sauce

½ cup honey
½ cup mayonnaise or salad dressing
1 teaspoon poppy seeds

Combine all ingredients in a small bowl. **Yield: 1 cup.**

Gruyère-Chicken Pizza

1 (8-ounce) carton sour cream
1 tablespoon all-purpose flour
1½ cups chopped cooked chicken
1½ cups (6 ounces) grated Gruyère cheese,
    divided
¼ teaspoon ground cumin
⅛ teaspoon hot sauce
1 clove garlic, minced
1 Crispy Pizza Crust
⅓ cup sliced ripe olives
¼ cup chopped green onions
2 tablespoons grated Parmesan cheese

Combine sour cream and flour in a large bowl, stirring well. Stir in chicken, 1 cup Gruyère cheese, cumin, hot sauce, and garlic. Spread chicken mixture over Crispy Pizza Crust. Top with olives, green onions, remaining ½ cup Gruyère cheese, and Parmesan cheese. Bake at 450° for 15 minutes or until cheese melts. **Yield: one 12-inch pizza.**

Crispy Pizza Crusts

1 package active dry yeast
1 cup warm water (105° to 115°)
3 to 3¼ cups all-purpose flour, divided
1 tablespoon olive or vegetable oil
1 teaspoon salt
1 to 2 teaspoons yellow cornmeal

Combine yeast and warm water in a 2-cup liquid measuring cup; let stand 5 minutes. Combine yeast mixture, 1½ cups flour, oil, and salt in a large mixing bowl; beat at medium speed of an electric mixer until mixture is well blended. Gradually stir in enough of remaining flour to make a firm dough.

Turn dough out onto a lightly floured surface, and knead until smooth and elastic (about 5 minutes). Place in a well-greased bowl, turning to grease top. Cover and let rise in a warm place (85°), free from drafts, 1 hour or until dough is doubled in bulk.

Punch dough down; divide in half. Roll each portion to a 12-inch circle on a lightly floured surface. Transfer dough to 2 ungreased 12-inch pizza pans sprinkled with cornmeal. Fold over edges of dough, and pinch to form a rim; prick with a fork. Bake at 450° for 5 minutes for soft crust or 10 minutes for crisper crust. **Yield: two 12-inch pizza crusts.**

Note: Baked Crispy Pizza Crusts may be wrapped tightly and frozen up to one month. To use, remove from freezer, and let stand 30 minutes. Remove wrapping, and top as directed above with chicken mixture and Gruyère cheese.

Chicken Nachos

4 skinned and boned chicken breast halves
1 teaspoon salt
1½ teaspoons ground cumin
2 tablespoons butter or margarine
½ cup diced onion
¼ cup diced green pepper
1 (4.5-ounce) can chopped green chiles, undrained
⅔ cup chopped tomato
1 teaspoon ground cumin
¼ teaspoon salt
⅛ teaspoon pepper
About 3 dozen round tortilla chips
3 cups (12 ounces) shredded Monterey Jack cheese
¾ cup sour cream
About 3 dozen jalapeño pepper slices
Paprika (optional)

Combine chicken and 1 teaspoon salt in a large saucepan; cover with water. Bring to a boil; cover, reduce heat, and simmer 8 minutes. Drain chicken, reserving ⅔ cup broth.

Place chicken and 1½ teaspoons cumin in container of food processor; process until coarsely ground. Set aside.

Melt butter in a large skillet over medium heat. Add onion and green pepper; cook, stirring constantly, until tender. Add chicken, reserved broth, chiles, and next 4 ingredients; simmer, uncovered, 10 minutes or until liquid evaporates.

Place tortilla chips on baking sheets, and spoon about 1 tablespoon chicken mixture on each. Top each nacho with 1 heaping tablespoon cheese.

Broil nachos 5 inches from heat (with electric oven door partially opened) until cheese melts. Remove from oven, and top each nacho with 1 teaspoon sour cream and a jalapeño pepper slice. Sprinkle with paprika, if desired, and broil 30 seconds. Serve immediately. **Yield: about 3 dozen.**

Cheesy Chicken-Tortilla Stack

½ cup vegetable oil
6 (8-inch) flour tortillas
1 (8-ounce) carton sour cream
½ teaspoon seasoned salt
½ teaspoon hot sauce
2½ cups shredded cooked chicken
2½ cups (10 ounces) shredded Monterey Jack cheese
1¼ cups (5 ounces) shredded Longhorn cheese
½ cup plus 2 tablespoons minced green onions
1½ tablespoons butter or margarine, melted
⅓ cup shredded lettuce
¼ cup chopped tomato

Heat oil to 375° in a 10-inch skillet. Fry tortillas, one at a time, in hot oil 3 to 5 seconds on each side or until tortillas hold their shape and begin to crisp. Drain tortillas well on paper towels; set aside.

Combine sour cream, seasoned salt, and hot sauce. Place 1 tortilla on a lightly greased baking sheet; spread about 1 tablespoon sour cream mixture over tortilla. Sprinkle with ½ cup shredded chicken, ½ cup Monterey Jack cheese, ¼ cup Longhorn cheese, and 2 tablespoons green onions. Repeat all layers 4 times. Top with remaining tortilla. Reserve remaining sour cream mixture. Brush top tortilla and edges of tortillas with melted butter.

Cover with foil; bake at 400° for 25 minutes. Immediately remove foil after baking; place tortilla stack on serving plate. Spread remaining sour cream mixture on top tortilla; sprinkle with shredded lettuce and chopped tomato. Cut into wedges, and serve immediately. **Yield: 4 servings.**

Peppery Chicken in Pita

Peppery Chicken in Pita

6 skinned and boned chicken breast halves
   (about 1½ pounds)
¼ cup teriyaki sauce
1 teaspoon dried thyme
1 teaspoon ground white pepper
1 teaspoon black pepper
½ teaspoon garlic powder
½ teaspoon ground red pepper
2 tablespoons olive oil, divided
⅓ cup mayonnaise or salad dressing
1 tablespoon prepared horseradish
6 (8-inch) pita bread rounds
2 cups shredded lettuce

Cut chicken lengthwise into ½-inch-wide strips, and place in a shallow dish. Pour teriyaki sauce over chicken; cover and marinate in refrigerator 2 hours.

Remove chicken from marinade, discarding marinade. Combine thyme and next 4 ingredients; sprinkle evenly over chicken.

Heat 1 tablespoon olive oil in a large skillet over medium-high heat. Cook half of chicken 5 to 7 minutes, turning once. Drain on paper towels. Repeat procedure with remaining olive oil and chicken.

Combine mayonnaise and horseradish. Spread each pita round with about 1 tablespoon mayonnaise mixture; sprinkle evenly with lettuce, and top with chicken. Fold two sides of pita over chicken, and secure with a wooden pick. **Yield: 6 servings.**

Note: Before spreading pita rounds with mayonnaise mixture, wrap in heavy-duty plastic wrap, and microwave at HIGH 45 seconds or until thoroughly heated. This will prevent bread from cracking before folding.

Marinated Chicken in a Sandwich

8 skinned and boned chicken breast halves
1 cup soy sauce
½ cup pineapple juice
¼ cup sherry
¼ cup firmly packed brown sugar
¾ teaspoon minced fresh garlic
8 slices Monterey Jack cheese
8 Kaiser rolls, sliced in half horizontally
Mustard Sauce
Leaf lettuce

Place chicken in a large shallow dish. Combine soy sauce and next 4 ingredients, mixing well. Set aside ½ cup marinade and pour remainder over chicken. Cover and marinate in refrigerator 30 minutes. Remove from marinade; discard marinade.

Cook chicken, covered, over medium coals (300° to 350°) 15 minutes or until done, turning and basting with reserved marinade approximately every 5 minutes. Place slice of cheese on each chicken breast, and grill 2 additional minutes or until cheese melts. Remove chicken from grill.

Spread each side of rolls with Mustard Sauce; place chicken breast on bottom half of each roll; top with lettuce. Cover with roll top, and serve immediately. **Yield: 8 servings.**

Mustard Sauce

½ cup dry mustard
⅔ cup white vinegar
⅔ cup sugar
1 large egg

Combine all ingredients in container of an electric blender and blend until smooth.

Cook mixture in a heavy saucepan over medium heat, stirring constantly, about 7 minutes or until smooth and thickened. Store in an airtight container in refrigerator. **Yield: 1⅓ cups.**

Open-Faced Chicken Sandwiches

2 tablespoons butter or margarine
2 tablespoons all-purpose flour
1 cup milk
½ teaspoon salt
⅛ teaspoon white pepper
½ cup (2 ounces) shredded Cheddar cheese
1 pound sliced cooked chicken
4 slices sandwich bread, toasted
8 slices bacon, cooked, drained, and crumbled
¼ cup grated Parmesan cheese

Melt butter in a heavy saucepan over low heat; add flour, stirring until smooth. Cook, stirring constantly, 1 minute. Gradually add milk; cook over medium heat, stirring constantly, until thickened and bubbly. Add salt, pepper, and Cheddar cheese, stirring until cheese melts.

Place chicken on toast, and cover with sauce. Sprinkle with bacon and Parmesan cheese. Bake at 400° for 10 minutes. **Yield: 4 servings.**

Chicken Crêpes

3 cups finely chopped cooked chicken
1½ cups freshly grated Parmesan cheese, divided
1 tablespoon butter or margarine
¼ pound finely chopped fresh mushrooms
½ teaspoon salt
¼ teaspoon pepper
¼ teaspoon ground nutmeg
⅓ cup butter or margarine
⅓ cup all-purpose flour
3 cups milk
1 cup whipping cream
Basic Crêpes

Combine chicken and 1 cup cheese in a large bowl; set aside.

Melt 1 tablespoon butter in a medium skillet. Add mushrooms; cook, stirring constantly, until tender.

Stir in salt, pepper, and nutmeg. Set aside.

Melt ⅓ cup butter in a heavy saucepan over low heat; add flour and cook, stirring constantly, 1 minute. Gradually add milk; cook over medium heat, stirring constantly, until thickened and bubbly. Stir in whipping cream.

Add mushroom mixture and ⅔ cup sauce to chicken mixture, stirring well. Spoon ⅓ cup mixture into center of each crêpe, and roll up tightly; place crêpes, seam side down, in a lightly greased 13- x 9- x 2-inch baking dish.

Pour remaining sauce over crêpes, and bake at 350° for 25 minutes. Sprinkle with remaining ½ cup Parmesan cheese, and bake 5 additional minutes. **Yield: 8 servings.**

Basic Crêpes

1 cup all-purpose flour
¼ teaspoon salt
1¼ cups milk
2 large eggs
2 tablespoons butter or margarine, melted
Vegetable oil

Combine first 3 ingredients, beating at medium speed of an electric mixer until smooth. Add eggs, and beat well; stir in melted butter.

Refrigerate batter 1 hour. (This allows flour particles to swell and soften so crêpes will be light in texture.)

Brush bottom of a 6-inch crêpe pan or heavy skillet lightly with oil; place over medium heat until hot.

Pour 2 tablespoons batter into pan; quickly tilt pan in all directions so batter covers bottom of pan. Cook 1 minute or until crêpe can be shaken loose from pan. Turn crêpe over, and cook about 30 seconds. Place crêpe on a dish towel to cool. Repeat with remaining batter.

Stack crêpes between sheets of wax paper, and place in an airtight container, if desired. Refrigerate up to 2 days or freeze up to 3 months. **Yield: 16 to 18 (6-inch) crêpes.**

Salad Sampler

Chicken salad is still in style but with some surprisingly different versions. You'll find new favorites here to serve for brunch, lunch, or a light supper.

Old-Fashioned Chicken Salad, Chicken-Fruit Salad, Poulet Rémoulade

Chicken Salad in Puff Pastry, Marinated Chicken-Grape Salad, Chicken Salad Oriental

Chutney-Chicken Salad, Aspic-Topped Chicken Salad, Dilled Chicken Salad

Broccoli-Chicken Salad, BLT Chicken Salad, Grilled Chicken Salad

Clockwise from top: Aspic-Topped Chicken Salad, Southwestern Chicken Salad, and Fruited Chicken Salad (pages 24, 38, and 29)

Old-Fashioned Chicken Salad

4 cups chopped cooked chicken
2 hard-cooked eggs, chopped
1 cup chopped celery
¼ cup chopped onion
¾ teaspoon salt
½ teaspoon celery salt
⅛ to ¼ teaspoon white pepper
Dash of red pepper
2 tablespoons lemon juice
½ to ¾ cup mayonnaise
Paprika
Garnishes: fresh parsley sprigs, cherry tomatoes

Combine first 9 ingredients; toss gently. Fold in mayonnaise; cover and chill 2 hours.

Spoon salad into a serving dish; sprinkle with paprika. Garnish, if desired. **Yield: 6 servings.**

Chutney-Chicken Salad

4½ cups chopped cooked chicken
¾ cup mayonnaise
½ cup chutney
1½ teaspoons curry powder
¼ teaspoon salt
1 tablespoon lime juice
1½ cups sliced almonds, toasted
Lettuce leaves
Garnish: apple slices

Combine first 6 ingredients in a large bowl; toss to mix. Cover and let chill thoroughly.

Stir in toasted almonds before serving. Serve salad on lettuce leaves. Garnish, if desired. **Yield: 6 servings.**

Aspic-Topped Chicken Salad

(pictured on page 23)

1 envelope unflavored gelatin
½ cup cold water
3 cups tomato juice
3 cups finely chopped celery, divided
2 tablespoons chopped onion
1 tablespoon Worcestershire sauce
Dash of salt
¼ teaspoon white pepper
1 envelope unflavored gelatin
¼ cup cold water
1 cup mayonnaise
1 cup whipping cream, whipped
3 cups chopped cooked chicken (about 6 breast halves)
Lettuce leaves

Sprinkle 1 envelope gelatin over ½ cup cold water; let stand 1 minute.

Combine tomato juice, 1 cup celery, and onion in a saucepan; bring to a boil, and cook 1 minute. Remove from heat; strain, discarding vegetables.

Combine vegetable liquid and gelatin mixture, stirring until gelatin dissolves. Stir in Worcestershire sauce, salt, and pepper. Pour mixture into a lightly oiled 11-cup mold; chill until the consistency of unbeaten egg white.

Sprinkle 1 envelope gelatin over ¼ cup cold water in a small saucepan; let stand 1 minute. Cook over medium heat until gelatin dissolves. Remove from heat; cool.

Fold mayonnaise and gelatin mixture into whipped cream. Fold in chicken and remaining 2 cups celery; gently spoon over aspic in mold. Chill until firm. Unmold aspic onto a lettuce-lined serving dish. **Yield: 8 servings.**

Dilled Chicken Salad

8 skinned chicken breast halves
1 teaspoon salt
1 cup chopped celery
3 hard-cooked eggs, chopped
1 (3-ounce) package cream cheese, softened
½ cup mayonnaise or salad dressing
¼ cup sour cream
1½ tablespoons chopped fresh dillweed
1 teaspoon dry mustard
¼ teaspoon salt
⅛ teaspoon pepper
Lettuce leaves
Slices of raw carrot and yellow squash

Combine chicken and 1 teaspoon salt in a Dutch oven; add water to cover. Bring to a boil; cover, reduce heat, and simmer 30 minutes or until tender.

Drain chicken, reserving broth for another use. Bone chicken, and cut into bite-size pieces. Combine chicken, celery, and eggs in a large bowl, and set aside.

Combine cream cheese and next 6 ingredients in a medium bowl. Add to chicken mixture, and toss well. Cover and chill thoroughly.

Serve salad on lettuce leaves with sliced carrot and squash. **Yield: 8 servings.**

Poulet Rémoulade

1½ quarts water
1 teaspoon salt
8 skinned chicken breast halves
1 cup shredded carrot
½ cup chopped celery
1 tablespoon minced fresh parsley
1 tablespoon chopped green onions
1 cup mayonnaise
1 tablespoon dry mustard
1 tablespoon cider vinegar
2 tablespoons olive oil
1 teaspoon paprika
1½ teaspoons prepared horseradish
½ teaspoon Worcestershire sauce
Dash of hot sauce
Garnish: carrot strips

Combine first 3 ingredients in a Dutch oven. Bring to a boil; cover, reduce heat, and simmer 25 to 30 minutes.

Drain chicken, reserving broth for another use. Bone chicken, and cut into bite-size pieces. Combine chicken, shredded carrot, celery, parsley, and green onions in a large bowl; set aside.

Combine mayonnaise and next 7 ingredients. Add to chicken mixture; toss gently. Cover and chill at least 3 hours. Garnish, if desired. **Yield: 6 to 8 servings.**

Quick Chicken for Salad

When time is short and your recipe calls for tender chunks of chicken, remember that chicken and the microwave are ideal partners. For 2 cups chopped cooked chicken:
• Arrange 4 skinned and boned chicken breast halves around sides of an 8-inch square dish. Pour ½ cup water over chicken and sprinkle with pepper.
• Cover with heavy-duty plastic wrap; vent corner. Microwave at HIGH 6 minutes or until juice is no longer pink.
• Let stand, covered, 5 minutes; drain. When cool enough to handle, chop chicken.

Chicken Salad in Puff Pastry

3½ cups chopped cooked chicken
1½ cups chopped celery
½ cup mayonnaise
⅓ cup honey mustard
3 tablespoons finely chopped onion
1 teaspoon salt
¾ teaspoon cracked pepper
½ teaspoon dry mustard
¾ cup slivered almonds, toasted
Puff Pastry Ring
Curly leaf lettuce

Combine chicken and celery in a bowl. Combine mayonnaise and next 5 ingredients; stir well. Add to chicken; toss gently. Stir in almonds.

Split Puff Pastry Ring in half horizontally; remove and discard soft dough inside. Line bottom half of pastry ring with lettuce; top with chicken salad. Replace pastry ring top. **Yield: 12 servings.**

Puff Pastry Ring

1⅓ cups water
⅔ cup butter
1⅓ cups all-purpose flour
¼ teaspoon salt
¼ to ½ teaspoon celery seeds
6 large eggs

Trace a 9-inch circle on parchment paper. Turn paper over, and place on a greased baking sheet.

Combine water and butter in a medium saucepan; bring to a boil. Combine flour, salt, and celery seeds; stir well. Add to butter mixture, all at once, stirring vigorously over medium-high heat until mixture leaves sides of pan and forms a smooth ball. Remove from heat, and let cool 2 minutes.

Add eggs, one at a time, beating thoroughly with a wooden spoon after each addition; beat until dough is smooth.

Spoon dough into a large pastry bag fitted with a large fluted tip. Working quickly, pipe into 12 rosettes on 9-inch circle on baking sheet. Bake at 400° for 40 to 50 minutes or until puffed and golden. Cool on a wire rack. **Yield: 12 servings.**

Chicken Salad in Puff Pastry Techniques

For a fancy pastry ring, pipe dough from a pastry bag, or simply spoon dough onto the parchment paper.

Cool on a wire rack, away from drafts. Carefully slice the cooled ring in half horizontally.

Remove the soft dough from inside of pastry before filling ring with lettuce leaves and chicken salad.

Chicken Salad in Puff Pastry

Chicken-Fruit Salad

Chicken-Fruit Salad

1 small head Bibb lettuce
1 avocado
2 chicken breast halves, cooked and cubed
1 small apple, diced
1 small banana, sliced
1 (8-ounce) can pineapple chunks, drained
½ cup chopped pecans
⅓ to ½ cup mayonnaise or salad dressing

Remove 6 outer leaves of lettuce; tear remaining lettuce. Peel and seed avocado. Slice half of avocado and set aside; chop remaining avocado.

Combine torn lettuce, chopped avocado, chicken, and next 5 ingredients; toss gently. Serve on reserved lettuce leaves, and garnish with avocado slices. **Yield: 2 servings.**

Marinated Chicken-Grape Salad

⅔ cup dry white wine
3 tablespoons lemon juice
4 chicken breast halves, cooked and cut into strips
1 cup mayonnaise
¼ teaspoon salt
⅛ teaspoon white pepper
Red-leaf lettuce
1 cup halved seedless green grapes
1 cup halved seedless red grapes
1½ cups diagonally sliced celery
½ cup cashews

Combine wine and lemon juice; pour over chicken. Cover and chill 2 hours. Drain, reserving marinade. Strain marinade, reserving ⅓ cup. Combine reserved marinade, mayonnaise, salt, and pepper.

Line 4 plates with lettuce. Arrange chicken, grapes, celery, and cashews over lettuce. Serve with mayonnaise mixture. **Yield: 4 servings.**

Fruited Chicken Salad

(pictured on page 23)

4 cups chopped cooked chicken
2 cups diced celery
2 cups halved seedless red or green grapes
1 (15¼-ounce) can pineapple tidbits, drained
1 (11-ounce) can mandarin oranges, drained
1 cup slivered almonds, toasted
½ cup mayonnaise
½ cup sour cream
2 tablespoons lemon juice
¼ teaspoon salt
¼ teaspoon white pepper
Fresh escarole
Cheese Tart Shells

Combine first 6 ingredients, and toss well. Combine mayonnaise and next 4 ingredients; add to chicken mixture, stirring well. Chill.

Arrange escarole around inside edges of 8 Cheese Tart Shells; spoon chicken mixture on top. **Yield: 8 servings.**

Cheese Tart Shells

2 cups all-purpose flour
½ teaspoon salt
¾ cup shortening
1 cup (4 ounces) shredded Cheddar cheese
4 to 5 tablespoons cold water

Combine flour and salt in a bowl; cut in shortening with a pastry blender until mixture is crumbly. Stir in cheese.

Sprinkle cold water, 1 tablespoon at a time, evenly over surface; stir with a fork until dry ingredients are moistened. Shape into 8 balls; cover and chill.

Roll dough into 8 (6½-inch) circles on a lightly floured surface. Line 8 (4½-inch) tart pans with pastry; trim excess pastry.

Bake at 450° for 8 to 10 minutes or until lightly browned. **Yield: 8 tart shells.**

Asparagus-Chicken Salad

(pictured on page 2)

1 pound fresh asparagus
1½ cups chopped cooked chicken
3 cups iceberg lettuce, torn into bite-size
    pieces
¼ cup slivered almonds, toasted
¼ cup chopped parsley
1½ tablespoons raisins
1 red apple, unpeeled
Lettuce leaves (optional)
Italian Cream Dressing

    Snap off tough ends of asparagus. Remove
scales with a knife or vegetable peeler, if desired.
    Cook asparagus, covered, in a small amount of
boiling water 3 minutes. Plunge in ice water.
Drain well.
    Cut asparagus into 1½-inch pieces; reserve 8
pieces for garnish. Combine remaining asparagus,
chicken, lettuce, almonds, parsley, and raisins in a
large bowl. Cut half of apple into ½-inch cubes;
stir into chicken mixture. (Reserve remaining
apple for garnish.)
    Arrange salad in a lettuce-lined bowl, if
desired. Garnish with reserved asparagus and
apple slices. Pour Italian Cream Dressing over
salad. **Yield: 4 servings.**

Italian Cream Dressing

¾ cup sour cream
¼ cup crumbled Gorgonzola cheese or
    blue cheese
1 tablespoon lemon juice
¼ teaspoon garlic powder
Freshly ground pepper

    Combine all ingredients in a small bowl; stir
well. **Yield: 1 cup.**

Artichoke-Chicken-Rice Salad

2 (6-ounce) jars marinated artichoke hearts,
    undrained
1 (6.9-ounce) package chicken-flavored rice
    and vermicelli mix
2½ cups chopped cooked chicken
1 (6-ounce) can sliced water chestnuts,
    drained and chopped
1 (3-ounce) jar pimiento-stuffed olives,
    drained and sliced
1 cup chopped green onions
1 cup reduced-fat mayonnaise
1½ tablespoons curry powder
1 teaspoon pepper
Lettuce leaves

    Drain artichoke hearts, reserving marinade;
coarsely chop artichokes.
    Cook rice mix according to package directions;
stir in reserved marinade. Cool.
    Combine artichoke hearts, rice mixture,
chopped chicken, and next 3 ingredients.
    Combine mayonnaise, curry powder, and pepper;
stir into chicken mixture.
    Cover and chill 1 to 2 hours. Serve on lettuce
leaves. **Yield: 8 servings.**

Broccoli-Chicken Salad

4 cups chopped cooked chicken
¼ cup sliced pimiento-stuffed olives
1 pound fresh broccoli, broken into flowerets
⅔ cup mayonnaise or salad dressing
¼ teaspoon curry powder
Lettuce leaves (optional)

    Combine chicken, olives, and broccoli. Com-
bine mayonnaise and curry powder, stirring well;
add to chicken mixture, and toss well. Cover and
chill. Serve in a lettuce-lined bowl, if desired.
Yield: 6 to 8 servings.

Chicken Salad Oriental

½ **cup uncooked macaroni**
2 **cups chopped cooked chicken**
½ **cup sliced green onions**
1 **(8-ounce) can sliced water chestnuts, drained**
½ **cup mayonnaise or salad dressing**
2 **teaspoons soy sauce**
¼ **teaspoon ground ginger**
⅛ **teaspoon pepper**
2 **cups (¾-pound) fresh snow pea pods,**
blanched
½ **cup slivered almonds, toasted**

Cook macaroni according to package directions; drain. Combine macaroni and next 3 ingredients; toss well.

Combine mayonnaise and next 3 ingredients, stirring well; fold into chicken mixture. Cover and chill 2 hours.

Divide snow peas among 4 plates. Top with chicken salad, and sprinkle with toasted almonds. **Yield: 4 servings.**

Chicken Salad Oriental

BLT Chicken Salad

BLT Chicken Salad

½ cup mayonnaise
¼ cup commercial barbecue sauce
2 tablespoons grated onion
1 tablespoon lemon juice
½ teaspoon pepper
2 large tomatoes, chopped
8 cups torn leaf lettuce or iceberg lettuce
3 cups chopped cooked chicken
10 slices bacon, cooked and crumbled
2 hard-cooked eggs, sliced

Combine first 5 ingredients in a small bowl; stir well. Cover and chill dressing mixture thoroughly.

Press chopped tomato between several layers of paper towels to remove excess moisture.

Arrange lettuce on individual salad plates; top each serving with tomato and chopped cooked chicken.

Spoon dressing mixture over salads; sprinkle with crumbled bacon, and garnish with egg slices. Serve immediately. **Yield: 4 servings.**

BLT Chicken Salad Technique

This egg slicer makes slicing hard-cooked eggs a simple task; the slices make a pretty garnish.

Layered Chicken Salad

3 cups chopped cooked chicken, divided
2 cups torn lettuce
1 cup cooked long-grain rice
1 (10-ounce) package frozen English peas, thawed
¼ cup chopped fresh parsley
2 large tomatoes, seeded and chopped
1 cup thinly sliced cucumber
1 small sweet red pepper, chopped
1 small green pepper, chopped
Creamy Dressing
Red pepper rings

Layer 1½ cups chicken and lettuce in a 3-quart bowl. Combine rice, peas, and parsley; spoon evenly over lettuce.

Layer tomato, cucumber, chopped red pepper, green pepper, and remaining 1½ cups chicken.

Spoon Creamy Dressing evenly over top of salad, sealing to edge of bowl. Top with red pepper rings; cover and chill 8 hours. Toss before serving. **Yield: 8 servings.**

Creamy Dressing

1 cup mayonnaise
½ cup sour cream
½ cup raisins
½ cup finely chopped onion
¼ cup sweet pickle relish
2 tablespoons milk
½ teaspoon celery seeds
½ teaspoon dillseeds
½ teaspoon dry mustard
½ teaspoon garlic salt

Combine all ingredients; stir well. **Yield: about 2¾ cups.**

Chicken Tortellini Salad

1 pound boneless chicken breasts, cut into strips
2 cloves garlic, minced
2 tablespoons olive oil
1 (8-ounce) package tortellini with Parmesan
   cheese
2 tablespoons olive oil
3 stalks celery, chopped
1 medium-size red pepper, cut into strips
⅓ cup chopped purple onion
5 ounces smoked Gouda cheese, cut into strips
¾ cup olive oil
¾ cup cider vinegar
2 tablespoons honey
2 tablespoons Dijon mustard
1 teaspoon dry mustard
Bibb lettuce leaves
5 slices Canadian bacon, cut into strips
Garnish: celery leaves

Cook chicken and garlic in 2 tablespoons hot
oil, stirring constantly, until chicken is done;
drain and set aside.

Cook tortellini according to package directions;
drain well. Combine tortellini and 2 tablespoons
oil in a large bowl, tossing gently. Add chicken,
celery, red pepper, onion, and cheese.

Combine ¾ cup olive oil and next 4 ingredients in a jar; cover tightly, and shake vigorously.
Pour mixture over salad, and toss gently.

Serve salad immediately or chill. Arrange on
lettuce leaves, and top with Canadian bacon.
Garnish, if desired. **Yield: 6 servings.**

Warm Chinese Chicken Salad

¼ cup cider vinegar
2 tablespoons walnut oil
2 tablespoons vegetable oil
2 tablespoons chicken broth
1 teaspoon dried tarragon
½ teaspoon Dijon mustard
½ teaspoon Worcestershire sauce
¼ teaspoon salt
⅛ teaspoon ground nutmeg
2 cups torn Chinese cabbage
2 cups torn romaine lettuce
⅔ cup chopped walnuts, toasted
3 cups coarsely chopped cooked chicken
1½ cups halved seedless red grapes

Combine first 9 ingredients in a small bowl,
stirring well. Toss cabbage and lettuce with half
of dressing mixture in a large shallow bowl.
Sprinkle walnuts over cabbage mixture.

Combine chicken and 3 tablespoons remaining dressing mixture in a skillet over medium
heat. Cook, stirring occasionally, until chicken is
thoroughly heated.

Toss hot chicken mixture and grape halves
with cabbage mixture. Serve salad warm with
remaining dressing. **Yield: 4 servings.**

Wow! Chicken Salad

Today's chicken salad goes far
beyond being chunks of chicken
tossed with mayonnaise, celery,
and pickle relish. Pasta and chick-
en make a splendid partnership in
Chicken Tortellini Salad. And for
a casual cold weather salad, try
Warm Chinese Chicken Salad or
one of our hot chicken salads on
page 36.

Warm Chinese Chicken Salad

Hot Chicken Salad Casserole

4 cups chopped cooked chicken
1½ cups chopped celery
4 hard-cooked eggs, chopped
1 (2-ounce) jar diced pimiento, drained
1 tablespoon finely chopped onion
¾ cup mayonnaise
2 tablespoons lemon juice
¾ teaspoon salt
1 cup (4 ounces) shredded Cheddar cheese
⅔ cup sliced almonds, toasted

Combine first 8 ingredients in a bowl; mix well. Spoon into a lightly greased 12- x 8- x 2-inch baking dish; cover and bake at 350° for 20 minutes.

Sprinkle with cheese; top with almonds. Bake, uncovered, 3 additional minutes or until cheese melts. **Yield: 6 to 8 servings.**

Hot Mexican Chicken Salads

5 cups chopped cooked chicken
2 cups (8 ounces) shredded sharp Cheddar
    cheese, divided
1 (15-ounce) can red kidney beans, drained
1 large sweet red pepper, chopped
¾ cup finely chopped onion
½ cup sliced ripe olives
½ cup sour cream
½ cup mayonnaise
1 (4.5-ounce) can chopped green chiles
1 (1¼-ounce) package taco seasoning
Vegetable oil
6 (8-inch) flour tortillas
Garnishes: avocado slices, cilantro sprigs

Combine chicken, 1 cup cheese, and next 8 ingredients, stirring well. Cover and chill.

Pour oil to depth of ¼ inch into a large deep skillet; heat to 375°. Fry tortillas, one at a time, until crisp and golden. Drain on paper towels.

Spoon chicken mixture evenly onto fried tortillas. Sprinkle with remaining 1 cup cheese. Place on baking sheets.

Broil 4 inches from heat (with electric oven door partially opened) 30 seconds or just until cheese melts. Garnish, if desired. Serve immediately. **Yield: 6 servings.**

Hot Mexican Chicken Salads Techniques

Slice avocado by peeling top half of skin and holding bottom half intact. Cut and lift out thin wedges from top of avocado.

Broil salads briefly to melt the cheese topping without burning the shells. Garnish salads, and serve immediately.

Hot Mexican Chicken Salads

Southwestern Chicken Salad

(pictured on page 23)

4 skinned chicken breast halves
½ teaspoon salt
¼ cup mayonnaise
¼ cup sour cream
1 (4.5-ounce) can chopped green chiles,
    undrained
1 teaspoon ground cumin
¼ teaspoon salt
⅛ teaspoon pepper
¼ cup chopped onion
4 (8-inch) flour tortillas
1 cup (4 ounces) shredded Longhorn cheese
3 cups shredded lettuce
Garnishes: sour cream, diced tomato
Picante sauce

Place chicken in a large saucepan; add ½ teaspoon salt and water to cover. Bring to a boil; cover, reduce heat, and simmer 30 minutes or until chicken is tender.

Drain chicken, reserving broth for another use. Bone chicken, and shred into small pieces. Set aside.

Combine mayonnaise and ¼ cup sour cream, stirring well. Add chiles and next 3 ingredients, stirring well.

Combine chicken and onion; add sour cream mixture, stirring to coat well. Cover and refrigerate 2 hours.

Place tortillas on a baking sheet; sprinkle cheese evenly over each tortilla. Bake at 300° for 10 minutes or until cheese melts; transfer to individual serving plates.

Arrange lettuce on tortillas; top each with one-fourth of chicken mixture. Garnish, if desired. Serve with picante sauce. **Yield: 4 servings.**

Grilled Chicken Salad

4 skinned and boned chicken breast halves
3 tablespoons soy sauce
3 tablespoons butter or margarine, softened
3 (¾-inch-thick) slices French bread
⅓ cup olive oil
2 cloves garlic, crushed
1½ tablespoons lemon juice
2 teaspoons Dijon mustard
2 dashes of hot sauce
1 large head romaine lettuce, torn
¼ cup freshly grated Parmesan cheese
Freshly ground pepper

Place chicken and soy sauce in a heavy-duty, zip-top plastic bag; marinate 30 minutes in refrigerator.

Spread butter over both sides of bread slices; cut slices into ¾-inch cubes. Place on a baking sheet, and bake at 350° for 15 minutes or until croutons are crisp and dry. Set aside.

Remove chicken from soy sauce; discard soy sauce. Grill chicken, covered, over medium coals (300° to 350°) 5 minutes on each side or until done. Cool 5 minutes; slice crosswise into ½-inch-wide strips. Set aside.

Combine olive oil and next 4 ingredients in a large bowl; stir with a wire whisk until blended. Add chicken strips, tossing to coat. Add romaine, cheese, croutons, and pepper, tossing gently to combine. Serve immediately. **Yield: 4 servings.**

Great Grilled Salad

Grilled Chicken Salad, a popular restaurant item, can be prepared quickly at home. For an easier version of this salad, substitute commercial croutons and Caesar salad dressing.

Comfort Food

Down-home chicken classics, such as pot pies and chicken and dumplings, are some of life's greatest comforts. These home-cooked favorites bring us back to basics amidst everyday hustle and bustle.

Chicken Noodle Soup, Biscuit-Topped Chicken Pie, Brunswick Stew

Chicken-and-Sausage Gumbo, Chicken-and-Oyster Gumbo, Kentucky Burgoo

Chili-Chicken Stew, Country Chicken and Dumplings, Chicken-and-Rice Soup

Individual Chicken Pot Pies, Creamy Chicken-and-Broccoli Soup

Chicken Ragout with Cheddar Dumplings (page 52)

Chicken Noodle Soup

1 (3½- to 4-pound) broiler-fryer
8 to 10 cups water
1 bay leaf
1 tablespoon chopped fresh parsley
1¼ teaspoons salt
¼ teaspoon pepper
¼ teaspoon dried basil
⅛ teaspoon celery seeds
⅛ teaspoon garlic powder
4 medium carrots, chopped
1 small onion, chopped
1 cup uncooked fine egg noodles

Combine first 9 ingredients in a large Dutch oven. Bring to a boil; cover, reduce heat, and simmer 1 hour or until chicken is tender.

Remove chicken from broth; discard bay leaf. Remove skin, bone chicken, and dice meat; set aside.

Add carrot and onion to broth; cover and simmer 30 minutes. Add chicken and noodles; cook 15 additional minutes. **Yield: 2½ quarts.**

Chicken-and-Rice Soup

1 (3½- to 4-pound) broiler-fryer, cut up
   and skinned
2 quarts water
1 medium onion, chopped
2 stalks celery, thinly sliced
1½ teaspoons salt
1 to 1½ teaspoons pepper
1 bay leaf
1 cup uncooked long-grain rice
2 carrots, diced

Combine first 7 ingredients in a Dutch oven. Bring to a boil; cover, reduce heat, and simmer 45 minutes.

Remove chicken, reserving broth. Discard bay leaf. Set chicken aside.

Add rice and carrot to broth; bring to a boil. Cover, reduce heat, and simmer 20 minutes or until rice is tender.

Bone chicken, and cut into bite-size pieces. Add chicken to broth; heat thoroughly. **Yield: 2 quarts.**

Creamy Chicken-and-Broccoli Soup

½ cup sliced fresh mushrooms
½ cup chopped onion
¼ cup butter or margarine, melted
¼ cup all-purpose flour
2 cups half-and-half
1½ cups chicken broth
1 cup chopped cooked chicken
1 cup frozen chopped broccoli, thawed
½ teaspoon dried rosemary
½ teaspoon salt
¼ teaspoon dried thyme
¼ teaspoon pepper

Cook mushrooms and onion in butter in a medium saucepan over low heat until tender; add flour, stirring until smooth. Cook, stirring constantly, 1 minute.

Add half-and-half and chicken broth; cook over medium heat, stirring constantly, until mixture is thickened and bubbly.

Stir in chicken and remaining ingredients. Cover and simmer 10 minutes, stirring occasionally. **Yield: 1 quart.**

Soup's On!

When you have leftover chopped cooked chicken, store it in freezer bags, and freeze up to 1 month. The tender chunks of meat are then ready to use in salads or soups like our Creamy Chicken-and-Broccoli Soup.

Creamy Chicken-and-Broccoli Soup

Brunswick Stew

Brunswick Stew

8 skinned and boned chicken breast halves
1½ cups chopped onion
1 cup chopped green pepper
1 tablespoon vegetable oil
3 (16-ounce) cans tomatoes, undrained and
    chopped
1 (8-ounce) can tomato sauce
¼ cup sugar
3 tablespoons white vinegar
2 tablespoons Worcestershire sauce
2 tablespoons all-purpose flour
1 cup water
1 pound red potatoes, peeled and cubed
1 (16-ounce) can pork and beans
1 tablespoon hot sauce
1½ teaspoons salt
½ teaspoon ground turmeric
½ teaspoon pepper
1 (16-ounce) can whole kernel corn, drained
1 (16-ounce) can lima beans, drained

Place chicken in a large Dutch oven; add water
to cover. Bring to a boil; cover, reduce heat, and
simmer 20 minutes or until chicken is tender.

Remove chicken from broth, reserving broth
for another use. Let chicken cool. Chop chicken,
and set aside.

Cook onion and green pepper in hot oil in
Dutch oven, stirring constantly. Add chicken,
tomatoes, and next 4 ingredients.

Combine flour and 1 cup water, stirring until
smooth. Stir flour mixture into chicken mixture.

Add potato and next 5 ingredients; stir well.
Cover and cook over medium heat 20 to 30 minutes or until potato is tender, stirring occasionally.
Add corn and lima beans, and cook 10 minutes or
until thoroughly heated. **Yield: 4 quarts.**

Brunswick Stew Technique

Use a vegetable peeler with a swiveling blade to
peel the potatoes. The blade will conform to the
shape of each potato.

Chili-Chicken Stew

6 skinned and boned chicken breast halves
1 medium onion, chopped
1 medium-size green pepper, chopped
2 cloves garlic, minced
1 tablespoon vegetable oil
2 (14½-ounce) cans stewed tomatoes,
    undrained and chopped
1 (15-ounce) can pinto beans, drained
⅔ cup picante sauce
1 teaspoon chili powder
1 teaspoon ground cumin
½ teaspoon salt
Shredded Cheddar cheese, sour cream, diced
    avocado, and sliced green onions

Cut chicken into 1-inch pieces. Cook chicken
and next 3 ingredients in hot oil in a Dutch oven
until lightly browned.

Add tomatoes and next 5 ingredients; cover,
reduce heat, and simmer 20 minutes. Top individual servings with remaining ingredients.
Yield: 6 servings.

White Lightning Texas Chili

1 pound dried navy beans
4 (14½-ounce) cans ready-to-serve chicken
    broth, divided
1 large onion, chopped
2 cloves garlic, minced
1 tablespoon ground white pepper
1 tablespoon dried oregano
1 tablespoon ground cumin
1 teaspoon salt
½ teaspoon ground cloves
5 cups chopped cooked chicken
1 (4.5-ounce) can chopped green chiles,
    undrained
1 cup water
1 jalapeño pepper, seeded and chopped
    (optional)
Shredded Monterey Jack cheese
Commercial salsa
Sour cream
Sliced green onions

Sort and wash beans; place in a large Dutch oven. Cover with water 2 inches above beans; let soak 8 hours. Drain beans, and return to pan.

Add 3 cans chicken broth and next 7 ingredients; bring to a boil. Cover, reduce heat, and simmer 2 hours or until beans are tender, stirring occasionally.

Add remaining can of chicken broth, chicken, and next 3 ingredients. Cover and simmer 1 hour, stirring occasionally.

Serve with cheese, salsa, sour cream, and green onions. **Yield: 2½ quarts.**

Making a Roux

Roux, the basis of many authentic Louisiana recipes, should be stirred constantly until it reaches a rich, dark brown color.

Chicken-and-Sausage Gumbo

1 pound hot smoked sausage, cut into ¼-inch
    slices
4 skinned chicken breast halves
¼ to ⅓ cup vegetable oil
¾ cup all-purpose flour
1 cup chopped onion
½ cup chopped green pepper
½ cup sliced celery
2 quarts hot water
3 cloves garlic, minced
2 bay leaves
2 teaspoons Creole seasoning
½ teaspoon dried thyme
1 tablespoon Worcestershire sauce
½ to 1 teaspoon hot sauce
½ cup sliced green onions
¼ teaspoon salt (optional)
Hot cooked rice
Gumbo filé (optional)

Brown sausage in a Dutch oven over medium heat. Remove to paper towels, reserving drippings.

Brown chicken in drippings; remove to paper towels, reserving drippings. Measure drippings, adding enough oil to measure ½ cup. Heat in Dutch oven over medium heat until hot.

Add flour to hot oil; cook, stirring constantly, until roux is the color of chocolate (about 30 minutes). Add onion, green pepper, and celery; cook until vegetables are tender, stirring often.

Stir in water; bring to a boil. Return chicken to pan; add garlic and next 5 ingredients. Reduce heat; simmer, uncovered, 1 hour.

Remove chicken; return sausage to pan and cook, uncovered, 30 minutes. Stir in green onions; cook, uncovered, 30 minutes. Add salt, if desired.

Bone chicken, and cut into strips. Add to gumbo, and thoroughly heat. Remove bay leaves; serve gumbo over rice. Sprinkle with gumbo filé, if desired. **Yield: 8 servings.**

Chicken-and-Sausage Gumbo

Chicken-and-Oyster Gumbo

1 (5-pound) hen
2½ quarts water
2 teaspoons salt
¾ cup vegetable oil
1 cup all-purpose flour
2 large onions, chopped
¼ cup chopped fresh parsley
1 teaspoon whole allspice
1 teaspoon crushed red pepper
5 bay leaves
½ teaspoon pepper
2 (12-ounce) containers fresh oysters, undrained
Salt to taste
2 teaspoons gumbo filé
Hot cooked rice

Combine first 3 ingredients in a Dutch oven. Bring to a boil; cover, reduce heat, and simmer 1½ hours or until hen is tender.

Remove hen from broth, reserving 8½ cups broth. Remove skin, bone hen, and cut meat into pieces. Set aside.

Combine oil and flour in Dutch oven; cook over medium heat, stirring constantly, until roux is the color of chocolate (about 30 minutes).

Add onion and parsley to roux; cook 10 minutes, stirring frequently. Gradually add reserved broth to roux, stirring constantly.

Combine allspice, red pepper, and bay leaves in a cheesecloth bag; add to broth mixture. Add pepper; simmer 2½ hours, stirring occasionally.

Add chicken and oysters; simmer 10 minutes. Remove from heat, and discard spice bag.

Add additional salt, if desired. Stir in gumbo filé. Serve over rice. **Yield: about 3½ quarts.**

Kentucky Burgoo

1 (4-pound) broiler-fryer
1 pound beef for stewing, cut into 2-inch pieces
1 pound veal for stewing, cut into 2-inch pieces
1 stalk celery with leaves
1 carrot, scraped
1 onion, quartered
6 fresh parsley sprigs
4 quarts water
1 (10¾-ounce) can tomato puree
1½ tablespoons salt
1 tablespoon sugar
3 tablespoons Worcestershire sauce
1½ teaspoons pepper
½ teaspoon ground red pepper
4 large tomatoes, peeled and chopped
2 large onions, chopped
2 large green peppers, chopped
2 cups sliced celery
2 cups chopped cabbage
1 (16-ounce) package frozen lima beans
1 (16-ounce) package frozen sliced okra
2 (8¾-ounce) cans whole kernel corn

Combine first 14 ingredients in a large stockpot. Bring to a boil; cover, reduce heat, and simmer 3 hours. Remove from heat, and let cool.

Strain soup; return meat and stock to stockpot. Discard vegetables. Let chicken cool. Bone and coarsely chop chicken. Return chopped chicken to soup; cover and refrigerate 8 hours.

Skim off and discard fat from surface of soup; add tomato and remaining ingredients. Bring to a boil; cover, reduce heat, and simmer 1 hour.

Uncover; simmer 1 hour and 45 minutes to 2 hours, stirring frequently. **Yield: 5 quarts.**

What's Gumbo Filé?

Gumbo Filé, a seasoning used to thicken and flavor gumbo, is made from the ground dried leaves of the sassafras tree. Stir filé into a dish after it's removed from the heat—cooking makes filé stringy and tough.

Kentucky Burgoo

Double-Crust Chicken Pot Pie

6 skinned and boned chicken breast halves
1 medium onion, chopped
2 tablespoons butter or margarine, melted
1 cup sliced fresh mushrooms
¾ cup chopped carrot
1 stalk celery, chopped
¾ cup frozen English peas
¾ cup peeled, chopped potato
1 cup chicken broth
¼ cup Chablis or other dry white wine
½ teaspoon dried parsley flakes
¼ teaspoon ground white pepper
1 bay leaf
2 tablespoons cornstarch
2 tablespoons water
1 (10¾-ounce) can cream of mushroom soup,
    undiluted
½ cup sour cream
¾ cup (3 ounces) shredded Cheddar cheese
Celery Seed Pastry
1 egg yolk, lightly beaten
1 tablespoon half-and-half or milk

Cut chicken into 1-inch pieces. Cook chicken and onion in melted butter in a Dutch oven 5 minutes.

Stir in mushrooms and next 9 ingredients. Bring to a boil; cover, reduce heat, and simmer 15 minutes or until vegetables are tender.

Combine cornstarch and water, stirring until blended; add to chicken mixture. Cook over medium heat, stirring constantly, until mixture comes to a boil. Remove from heat. Remove bay leaf. Stir in soup, sour cream, and cheese.

Roll half of Celery Seed Pastry to ⅛-inch thickness on a floured surface. Fit pastry into a deep 2-quart casserole. Spoon chicken mixture into pastry.

Roll remaining pastry to ⅛-inch thickness, and place over chicken mixture; trim, seal, and flute edges.

Reroll pastry trimmings; make chicken-shaped cutouts. Dampen cutouts with water, and arrange on top of pastry. Cut slits in pastry.

Combine egg yolk and half-and-half; brush over pastry. Bake at 400° for 30 minutes or until golden. Shield pastry with aluminum foil to prevent excessive browning. **Yield: 6 servings.**

Celery Seed Pastry

3 cups all-purpose flour
2 teaspoons celery seeds
1 teaspoon salt
1 cup shortening
4 to 6 tablespoons cold water

Combine first 3 ingredients; cut in shortening with a pastry blender until mixture is crumbly.

Sprinkle cold water, 1 tablespoon at a time, evenly over surface; stir with a fork until dry ingredients are moistened. Shape dough into a ball; chill. **Yield: pastry for one double-crust pie.**

Double-Crust Chicken Pot Pie Techniques

Roll half of pastry to ⅛-inch thickness; fit pastry into a deep 2-quart casserole.

Brush pastry with an egg yolk and half-and-half wash to give finished crust a rich color and glossy sheen.

Double-Crust Chicken Pot Pie

Individual Chicken Pot Pies

Individual Chicken Pot Pies

1 cup chopped onion
1 cup chopped celery
1 cup chopped carrot
⅓ cup butter or margarine, melted
½ cup all-purpose flour
2 cups chicken broth
1 cup half-and-half
4 cups chopped cooked chicken
1 cup frozen English peas, thawed
1 teaspoon salt
¼ teaspoon pepper
Basic Pastry

Cook first 3 ingredients in butter in a skillet over medium heat until tender. Add flour; stir until smooth. Cook, stirring constantly, 1 minute.

Add chicken broth and half-and-half; cook, stirring constantly, until thickened and bubbly.

Stir in chicken, peas, salt, and pepper.

Divide Basic Pastry into 8 equal portions. Roll 4 portions of pastry into 10-inch circles on a floured surface. Place in 4 (6-inch) pie pans.

Spoon chicken mixture evenly into each of the prepared pie pans.

Roll remaining 4 portions of pastry to 7-inch circles on a floured surface. Place pastry circles over filling; fold edges under and flute. Cut slits in tops to allow steam to escape.

Bake, uncovered, at 400° for 35 minutes or until crust is golden brown. **Yield: 4 servings.**

Basic Pastry

4 cups all-purpose flour
2 teaspoons salt
1½ cups plus 1 tablespoon shortening
⅓ to ½ cup cold water

Combine flour and salt; cut in shortening with a pastry blender until mixture is crumbly. Sprinkle cold water, 1 tablespoon at a time, over surface; stir with a fork until dry ingredients are moistened. Shape into a ball; chill. **Yield: pastry for 4 (6-inch) pies.**

Biscuit-Topped Chicken Pie

1 (3-pound) broiler-fryer, cut up
1½ teaspoons salt, divided
1 cup chopped carrot
1 cup frozen English peas, thawed
2½ cups diced potato
¼ cup chopped celery
½ teaspoon white pepper
1 teaspoon onion powder
¾ teaspoon poultry seasoning
3 tablespoons all-purpose flour
1 (5-ounce) can evaporated milk
1 cup chopped fresh mushrooms
Biscuit Topping
Butter or margarine, melted (optional)

Place chicken in a Dutch oven; add 1 teaspoon salt and water to cover. Bring to a boil; cover, reduce heat, and simmer 45 minutes or until chicken is tender.

Drain chicken, reserving 2¾ cups broth. Set chicken aside. Add remaining ½ teaspoon salt, carrot, and next 6 ingredients to broth; cook 20 minutes or until vegetables are tender.

Combine flour and milk; add to vegetable mixture, stirring constantly, until mixture is thickened.

Bone chicken, and cut into bite-size pieces. Stir chicken and mushrooms into vegetable mixture. Spoon into a lightly greased 13- x 9- x 2-inch baking dish. Arrange Biscuit Topping rounds over chicken mixture.

Bake at 400° for 25 minutes or until biscuits are golden. Brush tops of biscuits with butter, if desired. **Yield: 6 to 8 servings.**

Biscuit Topping
½ cup shortening
2 cups self-rising flour
⅔ cup milk

Cut shortening into flour with a pastry blender until mixture is crumbly. Add milk, and mix well.

Turn dough out onto a lightly floured surface. Roll dough to ⅓-inch thickness; cut rounds with a 2¾-inch biscuit cutter. **Yield: 15 biscuit rounds.**

Country Chicken and Dumplings

1 (3- to 3½-pound) broiler-fryer
2 quarts water
2 stalks celery, cut into pieces
1 teaspoon salt
2 cups all-purpose flour
2 teaspoons baking powder
½ teaspoon salt
¼ cup butter or margarine, softened

Place chicken in a Dutch oven; add water, celery, and 1 teaspoon salt. Bring to a boil; cover, reduce heat, and simmer 1 hour or until chicken is tender.

Remove chicken from broth, and cool. Discard celery. Bone chicken, and cut into bite-size pieces; set aside chicken and ¾ cup broth. Leave remaining broth in pan.

Combine flour, baking powder, and ½ teaspoon salt; cut in butter until mixture is crumbly. Add ¾ cup reserved broth, stirring with a fork until dry ingredients are moistened. Turn dough out onto a well-floured surface, and knead.

Pat dough to ½-inch thickness. Cut dough in 4- x ½-inch pieces, and sprinkle with additional flour.

Bring broth to a boil. Drop dough, one piece at a time, into boiling broth, gently stirring after each addition. Reduce heat to low; cover and cook 8 to 10 minutes. Stir in chicken, and serve immediately. **Yield: 4 servings.**

Chicken Ragout with Cheddar Dumplings

(pictured on page 39)

2 cups diagonally sliced carrot
1 cup sweet red pepper strips
3 tablespoons butter or margarine
¼ cup all-purpose flour
2 cups chicken broth
1 cup milk
1 tablespoon lemon juice
½ teaspoon salt
½ teaspoon pepper
3 cups chopped cooked chicken
1 cup frozen English peas, thawed
2 cups biscuit mix
⅔ cup milk
¾ cup (3 ounces) shredded Cheddar cheese
1 (2-ounce) jar diced pimiento, drained

Arrange carrot and pepper strips in a steamer basket; place over boiling water. Cover and steam 8 minutes or until crisp-tender; set aside.

Melt butter in a large heavy saucepan over low heat; add flour, stirring until smooth. Cook, stirring constantly, 1 minute.

Add chicken broth and 1 cup milk; cook over medium heat, stirring constantly, until mixture is thickened and bubbly. Remove from heat. Stir in lemon juice, salt, and pepper. Add chicken, steamed vegetables, and peas, stirring gently. Spoon into a lightly greased 11- x 7- x 1½-inch baking dish.

Combine biscuit mix and ⅔ cup milk, stirring until dry ingredients are moistened. Stir vigorously 30 seconds. Turn out onto a lightly floured surface, and knead 4 or 5 times.

Roll dough into a 12- x 9-inch rectangle. Sprinkle with cheese and pimiento, leaving a ½-inch border; roll up jellyroll fashion, starting with a long side, and turn seam side down. Cut into 1-inch-thick slices, and place over chicken mixture.

Bake at 400° for 30 minutes or until golden brown. **Yield: 6 servings.**

Chicken à la King

6 skinned chicken breast halves
8 mushroom caps, sliced
1 green pepper, chopped
2 tablespoons butter or margarine, melted
¼ cup plus 1 tablespoon butter or margarine
¼ cup plus 1 tablespoon all-purpose flour
5 cups half-and-half, divided
¼ cup sherry
4 egg yolks
2 tablespoons sherry
1 tablespoon diced pimiento
1 teaspoon salt
¼ teaspoon white pepper
Diced pimiento (optional)
Cornbread or toast points

Place chicken in a Dutch oven; cover with water. Bring to a boil; cover, reduce heat, and simmer 25 minutes or until chicken is tender.

Remove chicken from broth; reserve broth for another use. Cool, bone, and chop chicken; set aside.

Cook mushrooms and green pepper in 2 tablespoons butter in a skillet until crisp-tender. Drain and set aside.

Melt ¼ cup plus 1 tablespoon butter in a Dutch oven over low heat; add flour, stirring until smooth. Cook 1 minute, stirring constantly.

Add 4½ cups half-and-half and ¼ cup sherry; cook over medium heat, stirring constantly, until mixture is thickened and bubbly.

Beat egg yolks until thick and lemon colored; add remaining ½ cup half-and-half. Gradually stir about one-fourth of hot mixture into yolk mixture; add to remaining hot mixture, stirring constantly.

Add chicken, sautéed vegetables, 2 tablespoons sherry, and next 3 ingredients.

Cook over medium heat, stirring constantly, until mixture is bubbly. Sprinkle additional diced pimiento over top, if desired. Serve over cornbread or toast points. **Yield: 8 servings.**

Roasted & Baked

You'll find great variety in this collection of roasted and baked chicken. From casual Oven-Barbecued Chicken to elegant Rosemary-Riesling Chicken, our choices range from simple to all dressed up.

Herb-Roasted Chicken, Wild Rice-Stuffed Chicken, Creole Chicken

Spicy Almond Chicken, Orange-Pecan Chicken Drummettes, Golden Fruited Chicken

Rice-Stuffed Roasted Chicken, Roast Chicken with Pineapple-Mustard Glaze

Oven-Barbecued Chicken, Crispy Walnut Chicken, Basil Chicken

Herb Garden Chicken (page 55)

Herb-Roasted Chicken

Herb-Roasted Chicken

2 tablespoons butter or margarine, melted
⅓ cup white vinegar
3 tablespoons lemon juice
3 tablespoons chopped fresh tarragon
2 tablespoons olive oil
1 clove garlic, minced
1 teaspoon salt
1 teaspoon freshly ground pepper
1 pound round red potatoes, unpeeled
1 cup diagonally sliced celery
1 (2-ounce) jar sliced pimiento, drained
¼ cup chopped fresh parsley
1 (5- to 6-pound) stewing chicken
Garnishes: fresh parsley, fresh tarragon

Combine first 8 ingredients in a small bowl, mixing well. Set aside.

Cover potatoes with water in saucepan; cook, covered, over medium heat 15 minutes or until tender. Drain potatoes; cool.

Cut potatoes into bite-size pieces. Add celery, pimiento, and ¼ cup parsley, tossing gently. Add 2 tablespoons tarragon-oil mixture, tossing to coat. Set aside.

Remove giblets from cavity of chicken, and reserve for another use. Rinse chicken with cold water; pat dry with paper towels. Fold neck skin over back; secure with a wooden pick. Lift wingtips up and over back, and tuck under chicken.

Stuff chicken with potato mixture. Close cavity with wooden picks or skewers; tie ends of legs together with string or cord. Place chicken, breast side up, on a roasting rack. Brush entire chicken with remaining tarragon-oil mixture.

Insert meat thermometer in breast or meaty part of thigh, making sure it does not touch bone. Bake at 375° until meat thermometer registers 185° (about 2 hours), basting frequently with tarragon-oil mixture. Let cool 10 to 15 minutes before slicing. Place on a serving platter; garnish, if desired. **Yield: 4 servings.**

Herb Garden Chicken

(pictured on page 53)

⅓ cup chopped onion
⅓ cup diced carrot
⅓ cup diced celery
1 tablespoon chopped fresh parsley
3 tablespoons Chablis or other dry white wine
1 (3- to 3½-pound) broiler-fryer
2 cloves garlic, peeled and halved
⅓ cup butter or margarine, melted
⅓ cup Chablis or other dry white wine
2 teaspoons chopped fresh basil
2 teaspoons chopped fresh oregano
2 teaspoons chopped fresh thyme
½ teaspoon salt
¼ teaspoon ground white pepper
Garnishes: basil, oregano, thyme sprigs

Combine first 5 ingredients in a small bowl; toss gently. Set aside.

Remove giblets and neck from chicken; reserve for another use. Rinse chicken with cold water; pat dry with paper towels. Rub skin of chicken with cut side of each garlic clove half.

Stuff chicken with garlic halves and reserved vegetable mixture. Close cavity with skewers; tie ends of legs together with string or cord. Lift wingtips up and over back of chicken, and tuck under chicken.

Place chicken, breast side up, on a rack in a shallow roasting pan.

Combine butter and next 6 ingredients in a small bowl; stir well. Brush chicken generously with butter mixture.

Bake, uncovered, at 375° for 1½ hours or until chicken is tender, basting occasionally with any remaining butter mixture. Place chicken on a serving platter. Garnish, if desired. **Yield: 4 servings.**

Wild Rice-Stuffed Chicken

1 (6-ounce) package long grain and wild rice
    mix
3 tablespoons butter or margarine, melted
½ teaspoon dried thyme, crushed
⅛ teaspoon onion powder
1½ cups seedless green grapes, halved
1 (3- to 3½-pound) broiler-fryer
Salt
2 tablespoons soy sauce
2 tablespoons white wine
Garnish: green grapes

Cook rice mix according to package directions. Add butter and next 3 ingredients; stir well.

Season cavity of chicken with salt; place chicken, breast side up, on a rack in a shallow roasting pan. Stuff lightly with half of rice mixture. Close cavity with skewers or wooden picks.

Bake at 375° for 1½ hours. Combine soy sauce and wine; baste chicken with mixture during last 30 minutes of baking.

Spoon remaining rice mixture into a lightly greased 1-quart casserole; bake in oven with chicken the last 15 to 20 minutes of baking time.

Place chicken on a serving platter, and spoon rice around it. Garnish with grapes, if desired. Yield: 4 to 6 servings.

Microwave Directions:

Cook rice mix according to package directions. Add butter and next 3 ingredients; stir well.

Season cavity of chicken with salt, and stuff lightly with half of rice mixture. Close cavity with skewers or wooden picks.

Place chicken, breast side down, on a microwave roasting rack in a 12- x 8- x 2-inch baking dish. Microwave at HIGH 3 minutes. Microwave at MEDIUM (50% power) 20 minutes. Turn chicken, breast side up.

Combine soy sauce and wine; baste chicken with soy mixture. Microwave at MEDIUM 25 to

30 minutes or until drumsticks are easy to move.

Spoon remaining rice mixture into a lightly greased 1-quart casserole. Microwave at HIGH 6 to 8 minutes or until thoroughly heated.

Place chicken on a serving platter, and spoon rice around it. Garnish, if desired.

Rice-Stuffed Roasted Chicken

2½ cups cooked brown rice
1 cup chopped apple
½ cup chopped dried prunes
½ cup chopped dried apricots
¼ cup chopped celery
¼ teaspoon garlic powder
½ teaspoon grated lemon rind
1 teaspoon ground ginger
¼ teaspoon salt
¼ cup butter or margarine, melted
1 (2½- to 3-pound) broiler-fryer
2 tablespoons butter or margarine, melted
¼ teaspoon paprika

Combine first 10 ingredients in a large bowl; mix well.

Place chicken, breast side up, on a rack in a shallow roasting pan. Stuff cavity lightly with brown rice mixture. Close cavity with wooden picks or skewers.

Combine 2 tablespoons melted butter and paprika; brush over chicken. Bake at 375° for 1½ hours or until tender.

Spoon remaining rice mixture into a lightly greased 1-quart casserole; bake in oven with chicken the last 15 to 20 minutes of baking time.

Place chicken on a serving platter, and spoon rice around it. Yield: 4 servings.

Creole Chicken

Creole Chicken

1   medium onion, sliced
8   cloves garlic, minced
¼   cup olive oil
½   cup orange juice
⅓   cup fresh lime juice
3   tablespoons Chablis or chicken broth
1   teaspoon sugar
1   teaspoon salt
¼   teaspoon pepper
1   teaspoon white vinegar
1   (3- to 3½-pound) broiler-fryer
Garnishes: lime slices, orange slices, fresh
     cilantro

Cook onion and garlic in olive oil in a medium saucepan over medium-high heat 2 minutes. Add orange juice and next 6 ingredients.

Bring to a boil. Remove from heat; cool. Reserve ¼ cup marinade, and refrigerate it.

Place chicken in a shallow dish or heavy-duty, zip-top plastic bag. Pour remaining marinade over chicken. Cover or seal, and refrigerate 8 hours, turning chicken occasionally.

Remove chicken from marinade; discard marinade. Dry chicken with a paper towel. Place on a lightly greased rack, and place rack in a broiler pan.

Bake at 400° for 15 minutes; reduce heat to 350°, and bake 1 hour to 1 hour and 15 minutes, basting with reserved ¼ cup marinade.

Cover chicken with aluminum foil after 1 hour to prevent excessive browning. Place on a serving platter, and garnish, if desired.
Yield: 4 servings.

Roast Chicken with Pineapple-Mustard Glaze

Roast Chicken with Pineapple-Mustard Glaze

2 (2½- to 3-pound) broiler-fryers, quartered
4 large cloves garlic, sliced
¼ cup butter or margarine, melted
¼ cup minced fresh parsley
1 teaspoon dried thyme
1 (20-ounce) can sweetened pineapple chunks
⅓ cup honey
¼ cup Dijon mustard
1 tablespoon cornstarch
Hot cooked rice
Garnish: fresh parsley sprigs

Place chicken, skin side up, on a rack in a roasting pan. Place garlic slices under skin of chicken.

Combine butter, parsley, and thyme; brush over chicken. Bake at 350° for 45 minutes.

Drain pineapple, reserving juice. Combine ¼ cup pineapple juice, honey, and mustard. Brush mixture over chicken, and bake 15 to 20 additional minutes.

Combine cornstarch, remaining honey mixture, pineapple, and remaining juice in a saucepan; cook over medium heat, stirring constantly, until thickened and bubbly. Boil 1 minute, stirring constantly. Serve chicken and sauce over cooked rice. Garnish, if desired. **Yield: 8 servings.**

Spicy Almond Chicken

3 tablespoons butter or margarine
1 (3- to 3½-pound) broiler-fryer, cut up and skinned
1 (14-ounce) jar red currant jelly
½ cup prepared mustard
½ cup slivered almonds
3 tablespoons brown sugar
2 tablespoons lemon juice
½ teaspoon ground cinnamon

Melt butter in a large skillet over medium heat. Add chicken, and cook about 10 minutes or until lightly browned on all sides.

Place chicken in a lightly greased 13- x 9- x 2-inch baking dish.

Add jelly and remaining ingredients to skillet; cook over medium heat until jelly melts, stirring occasionally. Pour over chicken.

Cover and bake at 350° for 30 minutes. Uncover and bake 10 additional minutes or until chicken is tender. **Yield: 4 servings.**

Chicken in Foil

1 (2½-pound) broiler-fryer, skinned and quartered
¼ teaspoon garlic salt
⅛ teaspoon paprika
1 large onion, cut into 4 slices
1 large potato, cut into 8 slices
2 carrots, scraped and cut into ¾-inch pieces
2 stalks celery, cut into ¾-inch pieces
1 (4-ounce) can sliced mushrooms, drained
1 (10¾-ounce) can cream of chicken soup, undiluted

Cut 4 (24- x 18-inch) pieces of heavy-duty aluminum foil.

Place a chicken quarter in center of each; sprinkle with garlic salt and paprika. Top evenly with onion and next 4 ingredients.

Spoon soup evenly over each portion. Seal each packet, and place on a 15- x 10- x 1-inch jellyroll pan.

Bake at 400° for 1 hour and 15 minutes or until tender. **Yield: 4 servings.**

Oven-Barbecued Chicken

½ cup all-purpose flour
1 teaspoon paprika
½ teaspoon salt
⅛ teaspoon pepper
1 (2½- to 3-pound) broiler-fryer, cut up
¼ cup butter or margarine, melted
½ cup ketchup
½ medium onion, chopped
2 tablespoons water
1 tablespoon white vinegar
1 tablespoon Worcestershire sauce
½ teaspoon salt
½ teaspoon chili powder
¼ teaspoon pepper

Combine first 4 ingredients; stir well. Dredge chicken in flour mixture.

Pour butter into a 13- x 9- x 2-inch pan. Arrange chicken in pan, skin side down. Bake at 350° for 30 minutes.

Combine ketchup and remaining ingredients, stirring well.

Remove chicken from oven, and turn; spoon sauce over chicken. Bake 30 additional minutes. **Yield: 4 servings.**

Barbecued Chicken Legs and Thighs

4 chicken legs, skinned
4 chicken thighs, skinned
¾ cup ketchup
⅓ cup firmly packed brown sugar
3 tablespoons Worcestershire sauce
2 tablespoons orange juice
1 tablespoon dried onion flakes
1 tablespoon prepared mustard
½ teaspoon garlic powder

Place chicken in a greased 13- x 9- x 2-inch baking dish; set aside.

Combine ketchup and remaining ingredients, and pour over chicken.

Bake at 350° for 1 hour, turning chicken once. **Yield: 4 to 6 servings.**

Crispy Walnut Chicken

3 cups crispy rice cereal
½ cup walnuts
½ cup butter or margarine, melted
1 teaspoon garlic powder
½ teaspoon salt
½ teaspoon pepper
3 pounds chicken pieces, skinned

Position knife blade in food processor bowl. Add cereal and walnuts; top with cover, and process until finely ground. Set aside.

Combine butter and next 3 ingredients; stir well. Dredge chicken in butter mixture and then in cereal mixture.

Arrange chicken in a 15- x 10- x 1-inch jelly-roll pan; pour any remaining butter mixture over chicken. Bake at 350° for 1 hour or until chicken is tender. **Yield: 6 servings.**

Crispy Walnut Chicken

Orange-Pecan Chicken Drummettes

1 (6-ounce) can frozen orange juice
    concentrate, thawed and undiluted
3 large eggs, lightly beaten
2 tablespoons water
1 cup all-purpose flour
⅓ cup finely chopped pecans
3 pounds chicken drummettes, skinned
⅓ cup butter or margarine, melted
Red Hot Sauce
Hot cooked rice

Combine first 3 ingredients, and set aside. Combine flour and pecans, and set aside.

Dip drummettes in orange juice mixture; dredge in flour mixture. Pour butter into a 15- x 10- x 1-inch jellyroll pan; arrange drummettes in a single layer. Bake at 375° for 25 minutes.

Spoon Red Hot Sauce over drummettes, and bake 30 additional minutes. Serve over rice. **Yield: 8 to 10 servings.**

Red Hot Sauce

2 cups ketchup
¾ cup firmly packed brown sugar
1 to 2 teaspoons hot sauce

Combine all ingredients, stirring until smooth. **Yield: 2½ cups.**

Cutting Wings into Drummettes

A drummette, the first section and meatier portion of a chicken wing, is cut to resemble a miniature drumstick. If you're short on time, the supermarket butcher can do the trimming and skinning, if desired.

Rosemary-Riesling Chicken

8 skinned chicken breast halves
Salt and pepper
2 tablespoons vegetable oil
¼ cup minced shallots or onion
2 cloves garlic, crushed
1 cup Riesling wine or other dry white wine
⅓ cup chicken broth
1 tablespoon minced fresh rosemary or 1
    teaspoon dried rosemary
1 cup whipping cream
Hot cooked rice

Sprinkle chicken with salt and pepper. Brown chicken in oil in a large nonstick skillet over medium-high heat.

Remove chicken from skillet, reserving drippings in skillet. Place chicken in a 13- x 9- x 2-inch baking dish.

Add shallots and garlic to drippings in skillet, and cook until tender. Add wine; cook over high heat, deglazing skillet by scraping particles that cling to bottom. Cook until wine is reduced to about ½ cup.

Add chicken broth; stir well. Bring just to a boil; pour over chicken in baking dish. Sprinkle with rosemary.

Cover and bake at 350° for 20 to 30 minutes or until chicken is tender. Place chicken on a serving platter.

Transfer juices and drippings in baking dish to skillet. Simmer until mixture is reduced to about ½ cup.

Add cream; cook over high heat, stirring constantly, 4 minutes or until mixture is thickened. Remove from heat, and pour sauce over chicken. Serve with rice. **Yield: 8 servings.**

Rosemary-Riesling Chicken

Golden Fruited Chicken

Golden Fruited Chicken

6 skinned chicken breast halves
1 teaspoon ground ginger
¼ teaspoon salt
⅛ teaspoon pepper
⅛ teaspoon dried rosemary, crushed
2 cups orange marmalade
¼ cup apple juice
¼ cup orange juice
8 ounces dried apricots (about 1¼ cups)
8 ounces golden raisins (about 1½ cups)
⅓ cup firmly packed brown sugar
Garnishes: rosemary sprigs, orange rind

Place chicken in a lightly greased shallow roasting pan. Combine ginger, salt, pepper, and rosemary; sprinkle over chicken.

Cook marmalade in a saucepan over low heat until softened. Stir in juices; pour over chicken. Bake, uncovered, at 375° for 20 minutes.

Remove from oven; add apricots and raisins to liquid in pan. Sprinkle entire mixture with brown sugar. Bake 30 to 40 additional minutes or until golden brown, basting frequently with pan juices.

Arrange chicken and fruit on a serving platter. Pour some of pan juices over chicken. Garnish, if desired. Serve immediately. **Yield: 6 servings.**

Golden Fruited Chicken Technique

Pour the marmalade and juice mixture over the chicken, coating well.

Baked Lemon Chicken

4 skinned chicken breast halves
⅓ cup lemon juice
½ cup butter or margarine, melted
1 teaspoon garlic powder
1 teaspoon poultry seasoning
½ teaspoon salt
¼ teaspoon pepper
Hot cooked rice (optional)

Place chicken in a lightly greased 11- x 7- x 1½-inch baking dish. Combine remaining ingredients except rice; pour over chicken.

Bake, uncovered, at 350° for 1 hour or until chicken is tender, basting frequently. Serve with rice, if desired. **Yield: 4 servings.**

Basil Chicken

½ cup dry white wine
¼ cup olive oil
¼ cup chopped fresh basil
2 cloves garlic, minced
Dash of hot sauce
4 skinned and boned chicken breast halves

Combine first 5 ingredients in a small bowl; reserve ¼ cup marinade and refrigerate. Place chicken in a shallow dish or heavy-duty, zip-top plastic bag. Pour remaining marinade over chicken. Cover or seal, and refrigerate 8 hours, turning chicken occasionally.

Remove chicken from marinade; discard marinade. Place chicken in a greased 8-inch square dish.

Bake at 350° for 10 minutes; turn chicken. Brush with reserved marinade, and bake 10 to 15 additional minutes. **Yield: 4 servings.**

Note: Chicken may be grilled 5 inches from hot coals for 5 minutes. Turn chicken; brush with reserved marinade, and grill 5 additional minutes.

Pecan Chicken

4 skinned and boned chicken breast halves
¼ cup honey
¼ cup Dijon mustard
1 cup finely chopped pecans

Place chicken between 2 sheets of heavy-duty plastic wrap; flatten to ¼-inch thickness, using a meat mallet or rolling pin. Set aside.

Combine honey and mustard; spread on both sides of chicken, and dredge chicken in pecans.

Arrange chicken in a lightly greased shallow baking dish. Bake at 350° for 30 minutes or until tender. **Yield: 4 servings.**

Parmesan Chicken

1 large egg, lightly beaten
1 tablespoon milk
½ cup grated Parmesan cheese
¼ cup all-purpose flour
1 teaspoon paprika
½ teaspoon salt
¼ teaspoon pepper
4 skinned chicken breast halves
3 tablespoons butter or margarine, melted

Combine egg and milk in a small bowl; stir well. Combine cheese and next 4 ingredients; stir well.

Dip chicken in egg mixture; dredge in flour mixture. Arrange chicken in an 11- x 7- x 1½-inch baking dish. Drizzle melted butter over top.

Bake at 350° for 40 to 45 minutes or until chicken is tender. **Yield: 4 servings.**

Note: Six large chicken thighs may be substituted for chicken breasts. Bake as directed for 35 to 40 minutes.

Crunchy Seasoned Chicken

½ cup sour cream
2 tablespoons lemon juice
1½ tablespoons Worcestershire sauce
1½ teaspoons celery salt
¼ teaspoon garlic powder
¼ teaspoon onion powder
⅛ teaspoon pepper
6 skinned chicken breast halves
1¾ cups saltine cracker crumbs (about 40 crackers)
1½ teaspoons paprika
2 tablespoons butter or margarine, melted
Garnish: lemon slices

Combine first 7 ingredients in a small bowl; mix well. Brush mixture on chicken, coating well.

Place chicken in a 13- x 9- x 2-inch dish; cover and refrigerate 8 hours.

Combine cracker crumbs and paprika; roll chicken in cracker crumb mixture, coating well.

Place chicken in a lightly greased 3-quart casserole. Drizzle with melted butter.

Bake, uncovered, at 350° for 1 hour or until tender. Garnish, if desired. **Yield: 6 servings.**

Roasting & Baking Tips

• To quickly coat chicken before baking, combine dry coating ingredients in a plastic bag. Add a few chicken pieces and shake until they are evenly coated.

• When stuffing a chicken, count on about ¾ cup dressing per pound.

• For safety, do not stuff a chicken until just before cooking.

Versatile Chicken Breasts

Whether on or off the bone, chicken breasts make any occasion special.
Simply sauced, shaped into rollups, or wrapped in pastry—
all offer great taste and eye appeal.

Creamy Almond Chicken, Champagne Chicken, Chicken Véronique

Chicken Breasts Lombardy, Fontina-Baked Chicken, Hearts of Palm Chicken Rolls

Dijon-Herb Chicken, Pesto-Stuffed Chicken Rolls, Chicken in Mushroom Sauce

Chicken Cordon Bleu, Spinach-Stuffed Chicken in Puff Pastry

Dijon Chicken with Pasta (page 71)

Quick Chicken

(pictured on cover)

Vegetable cooking spray
4 skinned and boned chicken breast halves
½ cup water
¼ teaspoon salt

Coat a nonstick skillet with cooking spray; place over medium heat until hot. Add chicken, and cook 12 minutes, turning once.

Add water and salt; cover, and simmer 5 minutes. Drain chicken, and serve with one of the following sauces or toppings. **Yield: 4 servings.**

Rainbow Pepper Topping

(pictured on cover)

1 small onion, sliced and separated into rings
1 clove garlic, minced
2 tablespoons olive oil
1 small sweet red pepper, cut into strips
1 small green pepper, cut into strips
1 small yellow pepper, cut into strips
½ cup dry sherry
1 tablespoon chopped fresh parsley
¼ teaspoon salt
¼ teaspoon pepper
Hot cooked pasta
Garnish: fresh parsley sprig

Cook onion and garlic in olive oil in a skillet over medium heat 1 minute. Add peppers, and cook, stirring constantly, 2 minutes.

Add sherry, parsley, salt, and pepper; simmer 2 minutes. Spoon pepper mixture over chicken and pasta; garnish, if desired. Serve immediately. **Yield: 4 servings.**

Note: For a more formal presentation, serve the chicken breasts and sauce over a curly pasta.

Basil and Cream Sauce

2 tablespoons chopped shallots
¼ cup chopped green onions
1 tablespoon butter or margarine, melted
1 cup half-and-half
⅛ teaspoon pepper
2 teaspoons dried basil or 2 tablespoons chopped fresh basil
2 slices bacon, cooked and crumbled

Cook shallots and green onions in butter in a skillet until crisp-tender. Add half-and-half; simmer 5 minutes or until cream is reduced and slightly thickened.

Stir in pepper, basil, and bacon. Spoon sauce over chicken, and serve immediately. **Yield: ½ cup.**

Chervil-and-Savory Sauce

¼ cup chopped onion
1½ teaspoons butter or margarine, melted
¼ cup dry white wine
½ teaspoon dried chervil
⅛ teaspoon salt
⅛ teaspoon dried savory
⅛ teaspoon pepper
½ cup plain yogurt

Cook onion in butter until crisp-tender. Add wine, and simmer over low heat until wine almost evaporates (about 5 minutes).

Add seasonings; gently stir in yogurt (at room temperature).

Cook over low heat, stirring constantly, until thoroughly heated (do not boil). Spoon sauce over chicken, and serve immediately. **Yield: ⅔ cup.**

Green Peppercorn Butter Sauce

½ cup butter or margarine, melted
2 tablespoons whole green peppercorns,
    drained
2 teaspoons lemon juice
2 teaspoons Worcestershire sauce
1 teaspoon Dijon mustard

Combine all ingredients in a small saucepan. Cook over low heat, stirring gently; do not boil. Spoon sauce over chicken, and serve immediately. **Yield: about ½ cup.**

Country Ham Sauce

½ cup diced cooked country ham
1 clove garlic, minced
1 teaspoon butter or margarine, melted
1 teaspoon white wine Worcestershire sauce
½ teaspoon lemon juice
¼ teaspoon paprika
⅛ teaspoon white pepper
½ cup sour cream

Cook ham and garlic in butter 2 to 3 minutes. Stir in Worcestershire sauce and next 3 ingredients.

Fold in sour cream, and cook over low heat until thoroughly heated (do not boil). Spoon over chicken; serve immediately. **Yield: about ¾ cup.**

Chicken Curry Sauce

½ cup finely chopped onion
2 tablespoons butter or margarine, melted
1 (10¾-ounce) can cream of chicken soup,
    undiluted
½ cup half-and-half
1 tablespoon lemon juice
1 teaspoon curry powder
½ teaspoon ground ginger
Hot cooked rice
Condiments: chutney, toasted coconut, raisins,
    sliced green onions, and peanuts

Cook onion in butter in a saucepan until tender. Stir in soup and next 4 ingredients; cook over medium heat until thoroughly heated, stirring occasionally.

Spoon cooked rice onto a serving plate. Place chicken on rice, and spoon sauce over chicken.

Serve with several of the condiments. **Yield: about 2 cups.**

Team Chicken and Sauces

These six versatile sauces and toppings prove that good food often comes from the easy combination of just a few ingredients. These recipes honor simplicity and transform Quick Chicken into fast and fancy fare.

The sauces that accompany Quick Chicken call for a few carefully chosen ingredients that intensify taste and eye appeal. Follow our easy method of cooking the chicken breasts, prepare your choice of sauce, cook rice or pasta, and have dinner on the table in a flash.

Creamy Almond Chicken

⅔ cup sliced almonds
¼ cup butter or margarine, divided
6 skinned and boned chicken breast halves
⅛ teaspoon salt
⅛ teaspoon pepper
1½ cups whipping cream
1 tablespoon Dijon mustard
2 tablespoons orange marmalade
⅛ teaspoon red pepper
Hot cooked rice

Cook almonds in 1 tablespoon butter in a skillet, stirring constantly, until lightly browned. Set almonds aside.

Place chicken between 2 sheets of heavy-duty plastic wrap; flatten to ¼-inch thickness, using a meat mallet or rolling pin. Sprinkle chicken with salt and pepper.

Melt remaining 3 tablespoons butter in skillet over medium-high heat. Add chicken, and cook about 1 minute on each side or until golden brown.

Reduce heat to medium; add ½ cup almonds, whipping cream, and next 3 ingredients, stirring well.

Cook about 10 minutes or until sauce thickens. Sprinkle with remaining almonds; serve with rice. **Yield: 6 servings.**

Champagne Chicken

2 tablespoons all-purpose flour
½ teaspoon salt
Dash of pepper
4 skinned and boned chicken breast halves
2 tablespoons butter or margarine, melted
1 tablespoon olive oil
¾ cup champagne or dry white wine
¼ cup sliced fresh mushrooms
½ cup whipping cream

Combine flour, salt, and pepper; lightly dredge chicken in flour mixture.

Heat butter and oil in a large skillet; add chicken, and cook about 4 minutes on each side.

Add champagne; cook over medium heat about 12 minutes or until chicken is tender. Remove chicken, and set aside.

Add mushrooms and whipping cream to skillet; cook over low heat, stirring constantly, just until thickened. Add chicken, and cook until heated. **Yield: 4 servings.**

Chicken Véronique

¼ cup all-purpose flour
1 teaspoon salt
½ teaspoon pepper
8 skinned and boned chicken breast halves
½ cup butter or margarine
1 tablespoon currant jelly
⅔ cup Madeira wine
1½ cups seedless green grapes
Garnish: green grapes

Combine flour, salt, and pepper; dredge chicken in flour mixture.

Cook chicken in butter in a large skillet over medium heat until golden brown on each side. Cover, reduce heat, and cook 10 minutes or until chicken is tender.

Remove chicken to serving platter, reserving pan drippings.

Stir jelly and wine into pan drippings; cook until heated. Stir in grapes; cook just until heated. Spoon sauce and grapes over chicken. Garnish, if desired. **Yield: 8 servings.**

Dijon-Herb Chicken

8 skinned and boned chicken breast halves
¼ cup butter or margarine, melted
¼ cup lemon juice
2 tablespoons Worcestershire sauce
1 tablespoon Dijon mustard
½ teaspoon salt
2 tablespoons chopped fresh chives
2 tablespoons chopped fresh parsley

Cook chicken in butter in a skillet over medium heat 10 minutes on each side. Remove chicken to a serving platter, reserving pan drippings in skillet; keep chicken warm.

Add lemon juice and next 3 ingredients to pan drippings. Bring to a boil, stirring occasionally.

Stir in chives and parsley. Pour over chicken. **Yield: 8 servings.**

Tarragon Chicken

6 skinned chicken breast halves
½ teaspoon salt
¼ teaspoon pepper
1 tablespoon chopped fresh tarragon or
   1 teaspoon dried tarragon
½ cup diced onion
1 tablespoon butter or margarine, melted
1½ cups Chablis or other dry white wine
¼ cup water
⅓ cup whipping cream
2 tablespoons butter or margarine
2 tablespoons all-purpose flour
⅛ teaspoon pepper
Hot cooked rice

Place chicken in a lightly greased 12- x 8- x 2-inch baking dish; sprinkle with salt, ¼ teaspoon pepper, tarragon, and onion. Add 1 tablespoon butter, wine, and water.

Cover and bake at 350° for 1 hour or until chicken is tender. Remove to serving platter, and keep warm.

Pour drippings into a heavy saucepan. Bring to a boil, and cook until drippings are reduced to 1 cup; pour drippings into a small bowl. Add whipping cream; mix well, and set aside.

Melt 2 tablespoons butter in a saucepan over low heat; add flour, stirring until smooth. Cook 1 minute, stirring constantly. Gradually add whipping cream mixture; cook over medium heat, stirring constantly, until mixture is thickened and bubbly.

Stir in ⅛ teaspoon pepper. Serve chicken and gravy over rice. **Yield: 6 servings.**

Dijon Chicken with Pasta

(pictured on page 67)

6 chicken breast halves
¾ cup butter or margarine, softened
⅓ cup sliced green onions
¼ cup chopped fresh parsley
3½ tablespoons Dijon mustard
12 ounces uncooked fettuccine
Garnish: fresh parsley sprigs

Loosen skin from chicken, forming a pocket without detaching skin. Set aside.

Combine butter and next 3 ingredients, mixing well. Place 1½ tablespoons butter mixture under skin of each piece of chicken; reserve remaining mixture.

Place chicken, skin side up, in a lightly greased 13- x 9- x 2-inch baking dish. Bake at 350° for 1 hour, basting occasionally with pan drippings.

Cook fettuccine in a Dutch oven according to package directions; drain and return to pan. Add remaining butter mixture, tossing well. Serve with chicken. Garnish, if desired. **Yield: 6 servings.**

Chicken in Mushroom Sauce

Chicken in Mushroom Sauce

2 tablespoons sliced almonds
6 skinned chicken breast halves
1 cup plus 2 tablespoons Marsala wine, divided
1 (10¾-ounce) can cream of mushroom soup,
   undiluted
1 (6-ounce) jar mushrooms, drained
½ teaspoon pepper
1 cup (4 ounces) shredded Swiss cheese
⅓ cup herb-seasoned stuffing mix, crushed
¼ cup chopped fresh parsley
1 tablespoon butter or margarine
Paprika

Place almonds in a 9-inch pieplate. Microwave, uncovered, at HIGH 3 to 4 minutes or until toasted, stirring twice. Set almonds aside.

Place chicken in a shallow dish; pour 1 cup wine over chicken. Cover and marinate in refrigerator 1 hour. Drain chicken, discarding wine.

Arrange chicken on a 12-inch round glass platter or in a 13- x 9- x 2-inch baking dish with thickest portions toward the outside.

Combine remaining 2 tablespoons wine, soup, mushrooms, and pepper; spoon over chicken. Cover with wax paper, and microwave at HIGH 16 to 18 minutes, giving dish a half-turn at 5 minute intervals.

Sprinkle with cheese. Microwave, uncovered, at HIGH 1 to 2 minutes or until cheese melts. Combine stuffing mix and parsley; sprinkle over chicken.

Place butter in a 1-cup glass measure. Microwave, uncovered, at HIGH 20 seconds or until melted; drizzle over chicken. Microwave, uncovered, at HIGH 1 to 2 minutes or until chicken is tender.

Sprinkle with paprika. Top with reserved toasted almonds. **Yield: 6 servings.**

Chicken in Mushroom Sauce Techniques

Sliced almonds will toast slowly in the microwave. Be sure to stir them occasionally for even browning.

Arrange chicken breasts with the thick, meaty portions to the outside of a large-rimmed platter or a baking dish.

Top the chicken with a mixture of stuffing mix and parsley. Sprinkle with paprika and almonds before serving.

Chicken Breasts Lombardy

Chicken Breasts Lombardy

1 cup sliced fresh mushrooms
2 tablespoons butter or margarine, melted
8 skinned and boned chicken breast halves
⅓ cup all-purpose flour
⅓ cup butter or margarine, melted and divided
½ cup Marsala wine
⅓ cup chicken broth
¼ teaspoon salt
⅛ teaspoon pepper
½ cup (2 ounces) shredded fontina or
  mozzarella cheese
½ cup grated Parmesan cheese
¼ cup chopped green onions

Cook mushrooms in 2 tablespoons butter in a large skillet, stirring constantly, until tender. Remove from heat, and set mushrooms aside.

Cut each chicken breast half in half lengthwise. Place chicken between 2 sheets of heavy-duty plastic wrap; flatten to ⅛-inch thickness, using a meat mallet or rolling pin.

Dredge chicken lightly in flour. Place 5 or 6 pieces of chicken in 1 to 2 tablespoons butter in large skillet; cook over medium heat 3 to 4 minutes on each side or until golden.

Place chicken in a lightly greased 13- x 9- x 2-inch baking dish, overlapping edges. Repeat procedure with remaining chicken and butter. Reserve pan drippings in skillet. Sprinkle reserved mushrooms over chicken.

Add wine and broth to reserved pan drippings in skillet. Bring to a boil; reduce heat, and simmer, uncovered, 8 minutes, stirring occasionally. Stir in salt and pepper. Pour sauce evenly over chicken.

Combine cheeses and green onions; sprinkle over chicken. Bake, uncovered, at 375° for 20 minutes. Broil 6 inches from heat (with electric oven door partially opened) 1 to 2 minutes or until lightly browned. **Yield: 6 to 8 servings.**

Note: ⅓ cup white wine and 2 tablespoons brandy may be substituted for Marsala wine.

Fontina-Baked Chicken

½ cup all-purpose flour
¼ teaspoon dried oregano
¼ teaspoon pepper
¼ teaspoon paprika
¼ teaspoon poultry seasoning
⅛ teaspoon red pepper
2 tablespoons Parmesan cheese
6 skinned and boned chicken breast halves
2 large eggs, beaten
½ cup butter or margarine, divided
½ pound fresh mushrooms, halved
½ pound cooked ham, diced
2 cups (8 ounces) shredded fontina cheese,
  divided

Combine first 7 ingredients, mixing well. Dip chicken in beaten egg; dredge in flour mixture.

Melt ¼ cup butter in a large skillet over medium heat. Add chicken, and cook about 8 minutes on each side or until golden brown.

Remove chicken, and drain on paper towels. Place in a greased 12- x 8- x 2-inch baking dish or individual au gratin dishes.

Melt remaining ¼ cup butter in skillet. Cook mushrooms in butter, stirring constantly, 4 minutes or until tender; drain. Layer mushrooms and ham over chicken. Sprinkle with 1 cup fontina cheese.

Cover and bake at 350° for 35 minutes. Uncover; sprinkle with remaining 1 cup cheese, and bake 5 additional minutes. **Yield: 6 servings.**

Prize-Winning Chicken

Chicken Breasts Lombardy has long been a favorite at our *Southern Living* luncheons, and we've recommended it to many readers requesting an entrée for a special occasion.

Roquefort Chicken

1 cup fresh sourdough breadcrumbs
1 (1½-ounce) can grated Parmesan cheese
¼ teaspoon salt
¼ teaspoon freshly ground pepper
1¼ teaspoons dried thyme
3 tablespoons butter or margarine, melted
3 tablespoons olive oil
¼ cup milk
1 tablespoon white wine Worcestershire sauce
8 skinned and boned chicken breast halves
Roquefort Sauce

Combine first 5 ingredients in a pieplate. Combine butter, oil, milk, and Worcestershire sauce. Dip chicken in milk mixture, and dredge in crumb mixture.

Arrange chicken in a lightly greased 15- x 10- x 1-inch jellyroll pan. Bake at 350° for 30 to 35 minutes or until tender. Serve with Roquefort Sauce drizzled over chicken. **Yield: 8 servings.**

Roquefort Sauce

1 shallot, chopped
1 stalk celery with leaves, chopped
2 tablespoons butter or margarine, melted
½ cup white wine
1 (10¾-ounce) can condensed chicken broth, undiluted
1 cup whipping cream
2 tablespoons crumbled Roquefort cheese
1 tablespoon chopped fresh chives

Cook shallot and celery in butter over medium heat in a medium saucepan, stirring constantly, until tender.

Add wine and chicken broth. Bring to a boil, and cook over medium heat, stirring frequently, until liquid is reduced to about 1 cup (about 15 minutes). Strain.

Return broth mixture to saucepan. Add whipping cream, and return to a boil; reduce heat and simmer about 15 minutes or until mixture is reduced to about 1 cup, stirring frequently.

Remove from heat; add cheese, and stir until cheese melts. Stir in chopped chives. **Yield: 1 cup.**

Chicken Cordon Bleu

4 large chicken breast halves
4 (1-ounce) slices cooked ham
4 (1-ounce) slices Swiss or Gruyère cheese
Salt and pepper
2 tablespoons butter or margarine, melted
1 (10¾-ounce) can mushroom soup, undiluted
1 (4-ounce) can sliced mushrooms, drained
¼ teaspoon garlic powder
⅛ teaspoon curry powder
¼ cup Chablis or other dry white wine
½ cup sour cream
Whole wheat toast points
Garnish: fresh parsley sprigs

Loosen skin from chicken, forming a pocket without detaching skin. Arrange 1 slice each of ham and cheese under skin of each breast half; secure skin with wooden picks.

Sprinkle chicken with salt and pepper; place in an ungreased baking dish.

Bake, uncovered, at 375° for 30 to 40 minutes or until chicken is tender, basting with melted butter after 20 minutes.

Remove chicken from drippings; set aside, and keep warm. Pour pan drippings into a skillet, and cook over high heat until liquid is reduced to about ¼ cup.

Add soup, mushrooms, garlic powder, and curry powder; stir well. Cook over medium heat until thoroughly heated. Stir in wine and sour cream. Remove from heat.

Remove wooden picks from chicken. Serve mushroom sauce with chicken over whole wheat toast points. Garnish, if desired. **Yield: 4 servings.**

Chicken Cordon Bleu

Hearts of Palm Chicken Rolls

12 skinned and boned chicken breast halves
½ teaspoon salt
½ teaspoon white pepper
¼ cup butter or margarine, melted
2 (14.4-ounce) cans hearts of palm, drained
Béarnaise Sauce
Garnish: fresh tarragon sprigs

Place chicken between 2 sheets of heavy-duty plastic wrap; flatten to ¼-inch thickness, using a meat mallet or rolling pin. Sprinkle with salt and pepper; brush with butter.

Roll each piece of chicken around a heart of palm. Place seam side down on a lightly greased 15- x 10- x 1-inch jellyroll pan. Brush chicken rolls with remaining butter.

Cover and bake at 350° for 1 hour. Spoon Béarnaise Sauce over chicken rolls. Garnish, if desired. **Yield: 12 servings.**

Béarnaise Sauce

3 tablespoons white wine vinegar
2 teaspoons minced shallots
1½ teaspoons chopped fresh tarragon
    or ½ teaspoon dried tarragon
3 egg yolks
⅛ teaspoon salt
⅛ teaspoon red pepper
2 tablespoons lemon juice
½ cup butter or margarine

Combine vinegar and shallots in a small saucepan; bring to a boil over medium heat. Reduce heat, and simmer until half of liquid evaporates.

Strain vinegar mixture, reserving liquid; discard solids. Cool slightly; stir in tarragon. Set aside.

Beat egg yolks, salt, and pepper in top of a double boiler; add lemon juice, stirring constantly.

Add one-third of butter to egg mixture; cook over hot (not boiling) water, stirring constantly, until butter melts.

Add another one-third of butter, stirring constantly. As sauce thickens, stir in remaining butter; cook until thickened. Immediately remove from heat. Add vinegar mixture to sauce, stirring well. Serve immediately. **Yield: ¾ cup.**

Pesto-Stuffed Chicken Rolls

6 large skinned and boned chicken breast halves
¼ teaspoon salt
¼ teaspoon pepper
1 (3-ounce) package cream cheese, softened
¼ cup commercial pesto
½ cup finely chopped sweet red pepper
¾ cup corn flake crumbs
½ teaspoon paprika
Vegetable cooking spray
Garnish: fresh basil sprigs

Place chicken between 2 sheets of heavy-duty plastic wrap; flatten to ¼-inch thickness, using a meat mallet or rolling pin. Sprinkle with salt and pepper; set aside.

Combine cream cheese, pesto, and sweet red pepper in a small bowl, stirring with a fork until smooth. Spread 2 tablespoons over each chicken breast; roll up lengthwise, securing with wooden picks.

Combine corn flake crumbs and paprika; dredge chicken rolls in crumb mixture. Place in an 11- x 7- x 1½-inch baking dish coated with cooking spray.

Bake, uncovered, at 350° for 35 minutes; let stand 10 minutes. Remove wooden picks, and slice into 1-inch rounds. (An electric knife works best.) Garnish, if desired. **Yield: 6 servings.**

Note: Chicken Rolls may be prepared ahead. Prepare as directed above; do not bake. Cover and refrigerate overnight. Remove from refrigerator; let stand, covered, 30 minutes. Uncover and bake as directed above.

Pesto-Stuffed Chicken Rolls

Puff Pastry Pointer

Keep thawed pastry in the refrigerator until you're ready to use it. Dough is easiest to work with when chilled.

Chicken Rollups

1 (6-ounce) package wild rice-and-mushroom
   stuffing mix
6 large skinned and boned chicken breast halves
¼ teaspoon pepper
2 tablespoons butter or margarine, melted
2 tablespoons Dijon mustard
1¼ cups ground pecans
3 tablespoons vegetable oil
¾ cup chicken broth
¾ cup sour cream

Prepare wild rice-and-mushroom stuffing mix according to package directions. Set aside.

Place each chicken breast between 2 sheets of heavy-duty plastic wrap. Flatten to ¼-inch thickness, using a meat mallet or rolling pin.

Divide stuffing mixture evenly, and place on top of each chicken breast; fold sides of chicken breast over stuffing, roll up, and secure with wooden picks. Sprinkle with pepper.

Combine butter and mustard in a small bowl; stir well. Brush mustard mixture over chicken, completely coating all sides; roll in pecans.

Brown chicken on all sides in hot oil in skillet; drain and discard pan drippings. Add chicken broth to skillet; cover, reduce heat, and simmer 20 minutes.

Place chicken on a serving dish; keep warm. Stir sour cream into broth in skillet; cook over low heat, stirring constantly, until heated. Spoon over chicken. **Yield: 6 servings.**

Chicken Alouette

1 (17½-ounce) package frozen puff pastry
   sheets, thawed
2 teaspoons all-purpose flour
1 (4-ounce) container garlic-and-spice-
   flavored Alouette cheese
6 skinned and boned chicken breast halves
½ teaspoon salt
⅛ teaspoon pepper
1 large egg, beaten
1 tablespoon water
Garnish: kale leaves

Unfold pastry sheets, and sprinkle each with 1 teaspoon flour. Roll each sheet into a 14- x 12-inch rectangle on a lightly floured surface.

Cut one sheet into 4 (7- x 6-inch) rectangles; cut second sheet into 2 (7- x 6-inch) rectangles and 1 (14- x 6-inch) rectangle.

Set large rectangle aside. Shape each small rectangle into an oval by trimming off corners. Spread pastry ovals evenly with cheese.

Sprinkle chicken with salt and pepper, and place one in center of each pastry oval. Lightly moisten pastry edges with water. Fold ends over chicken; fold sides over, and press to seal.

Place each bundle, seam side down, on a lightly greased baking sheet.

Cut remaining large pastry rectangle into 24 (14- x ¼-inch) strips. Twist 2 strips together, and place crosswise over chicken bundles, trimming and reserving excess braid. Twist 2 additional strips, and place lengthwise over bundle, trimming and tucking ends under. Repeat procedure with remaining strips.

Cover and refrigerate up to 2 hours, if desired.

Combine egg and 1 tablespoon water; brush over pastry bundles. Bake at 400° on lower oven rack 25 minutes or until bundles are golden brown. Garnish, if desired. **Yield: 6 servings.**

Note: ½ cup chives-and-onion-flavored cream cheese may be substituted for Alouette cheese.

Chicken Alouette

Spinach-Stuffed Chicken in Puff Pastry

Spinach-Stuffed Chicken in Puff Pastry

4 skinned and boned chicken breast halves
½ teaspoon salt
½ teaspoon pepper
1 (10-ounce) package frozen spinach, thawed and drained
¾ cup (3 ounces) shredded Gruyère or Swiss cheese
½ cup finely chopped prosciutto or cooked ham (about 3 ounces)
¼ teaspoon salt
⅛ teaspoon pepper
Dash of ground nutmeg
1 (17¼-ounce) package frozen puff pastry sheets, thawed
1 large egg, lightly beaten
1 teaspoon water
1 (0.9-ounce) package béarnaise sauce mix

Place chicken between two sheets of heavy-duty plastic wrap; flatten to ⅛-inch thickness, using a meat mallet or rolling pin. Sprinkle chicken with ½ teaspoon each of salt and pepper.

Combine spinach and next 5 ingredients; shape into 4 balls, placing 1 in center of each chicken breast. Fold chicken over spinach.

Roll each sheet of puff pastry into a 12-inch square. Cut a 1-inch strip from side of each sheet, setting aside for garnish. Cut each sheet in half, making 4 (5½- x 6-inch) rectangles.

Place stuffed chicken breasts in center of pastry rectangles; fold sides over chicken. Combine egg and water, and brush on pastry seams, pinching to seal. Place seam side down on a lightly greased 15- x 10- x 1-inch jellyroll pan.

Cut decorative stems and leaves or desired shapes from reserved pastry strips. Brush back of cutouts with egg mixture, and arrange on chicken bundles.

Chill bundles and remaining egg mixture 1 hour. Brush bundles with egg mixture, and bake at 400° for 20 to 25 minutes or until golden.

Prepare béarnaise sauce according to package directions. Spoon 2 tablespoons sauce in each plate; top with bundle. **Yield: 4 servings.**

Spinach-Stuffed Chicken in Puff Pastry Techniques

Flatten chicken with a meat mallet; form spinach mixture into balls, and place in center of each breast.

Fold chicken over spinach; invert onto a cut rectangle of pastry. Fold ends of pastry over chicken.

Brush seams with egg mixture; press edges to seal. Make cutouts from reserved pastry; apply to bundles.

Chicken Breasts in Phyllo Pastry

1 cup mayonnaise or salad dressing
⅔ cup chopped green onions
3½ tablespoons fresh lemon juice
1 small clove garlic, minced
¾ teaspoon dried tarragon
8 skinned and boned chicken breast halves
¼ teaspoon salt
⅛ teaspoon pepper
16 sheets commercial frozen phyllo pastry, thawed
Butter-flavored vegetable cooking spray
3½ tablespoons grated Parmesan cheese

Combine first 5 ingredients in a small bowl; set aside.

Sprinkle chicken with salt and pepper. Place one sheet of phyllo pastry on a sheet of plastic wrap; spray evenly with cooking spray. Place another sheet of phyllo on top; spray with cooking spray.

Spread about 3 tablespoons mayonnaise mixture on both sides of 1 chicken breast; place breast diagonally in one corner of stacked pastry sheets. Fold corner over breast; fold sides over, and carefully roll up in pastry. Place seam side down in an ungreased 15- x 10- x 1-inch jellyroll pan.

Repeat procedure with remaining phyllo, cooking spray, mayonnaise mixture, and chicken breasts. Spray tops of pastry bundles with cooking spray; sprinkle with Parmesan cheese.

Bake at 350° for 40 to 45 minutes or until chicken breasts are done. Serve immediately.
Yield: 8 servings.

Note: Melted butter or margarine may be substituted for butter-flavored cooking spray.

Chicken and Vegetables en Papillote

6 skinned and boned chicken breast halves
¼ cup orange juice
¼ cup teriyaki sauce
1½ tablespoons sesame oil
½ teaspoon grated fresh gingerroot
2 to 3 tablespoons vegetable oil
6 green onions, chopped
2 medium carrots, cut into very thin strips
2 small yellow squash, thinly sliced

Place chicken between 2 sheets of heavy-duty plastic wrap. Flatten chicken to ¼-inch thickness, using a meat mallet or rolling pin. Combine orange juice and next 3 ingredients; reserve 3 tablespoons marinade, and refrigerate.

Place chicken in a shallow dish; pour remaining marinade over chicken. Cover and refrigerate 30 minutes, turning occasionally.

Cut six 15- x 12-inch pieces parchment paper or aluminum foil; fold in half lengthwise, creasing firmly. Trim each into a large heart shape. Place hearts on baking sheets. Brush one side of each heart with vegetable oil, leaving edges ungreased.

Remove chicken from marinade, and discard marinade; place a chicken breast half on one half of each parchment heart near the crease.

Arrange vegetables over chicken. Spoon reserved 3 tablespoons marinade over vegetables.

Fold over remaining halves of parchment hearts. Starting with rounded edge of each heart, pleat and crimp edges together to make a seal. Twist end tightly to seal.

Bake at 350° for 20 minutes or until bags are puffed and lightly browned and chicken is done.
Yield: 6 servings.

Chicken Combos

Ways to combine chicken with other ingredients are limited only by your imagination. To get you started creating your own combinations, we've included some of our tastiest "chicken and …" dishes.

Chicken Divan Casserole, Creole Chicken and Grits, Chicken Pilaf

Tipsy Chicken and Dressing, Chicken Fettuccine Supreme, Country Captain Chicken

Creamy Chicken-and-Ham Medley, Shrimp-and-Chicken Casserole, Chicken Curry

Chicken-Wild Rice Casserole, Ginger-Nut Chicken, Chicken Lasagna

Creamy Chicken-and-Ham Medley (page 87)

Chicken Divan Casserole

Chicken Divan Casserole

4 skinned chicken breast halves
1 fresh rosemary sprig
½ teaspoon salt
¼ teaspoon pepper
2 tablespoons butter or margarine
¼ cup all-purpose flour
1 cup milk
1 egg yolk, beaten
1 cup sour cream
½ cup mayonnaise
½ teaspoon grated lemon rind
2 tablespoons lemon juice
½ teaspoon salt
¼ to ½ teaspoon curry powder
2 (10-ounce) packages frozen broccoli spears,
    thawed and drained
⅓ cup grated Parmesan cheese
Paprika

Place first 4 ingredients in a large saucepan; add water to cover. Bring to a boil. Cover, reduce heat, and simmer 15 to 20 minutes or until chicken is tender. Drain, reserving ½ cup broth. Discard rosemary.

Let chicken cool slightly. Bone and chop chicken; set aside.

Melt butter in a heavy saucepan over low heat; add flour, stirring until smooth. Cook 1 minute, stirring constantly. Gradually add milk and reserved broth; cook over medium heat, stirring constantly, until thickened and bubbly.

Stir one-fourth of hot mixture into egg yolk; add to remaining hot mixture and cook, stirring constantly, 1 minute. Remove from heat; stir in sour cream and next 5 ingredients.

Layer half each of broccoli, chicken, and sauce in a greased 2-quart casserole. Repeat layers. Sprinkle with Parmesan cheese.

Bake, uncovered, at 350° for 30 to 35 minutes. Sprinkle with paprika. **Yield: 4 to 6 servings.**

Creamy Chicken-and-Ham Medley

(pictured on page 85)

1 tablespoon butter or margarine
½ cup sliced fresh mushrooms
⅓ cup butter or margarine
⅓ cup all-purpose flour
2½ to 3 cups milk, divided
1 cup whipping cream
1 cup freshly grated Parmesan cheese
½ teaspoon salt
¼ teaspoon pepper
¼ teaspoon ground nutmeg
Dash of ground red pepper
2 cups chopped cooked chicken
2 cups chopped cooked ham
2 (10-ounce) packages frozen puff pastry
    shells, baked
Paprika

Melt 1 tablespoon butter in a large saucepan over medium heat; add mushrooms, and cook, stirring constantly, until tender. Remove from saucepan; set aside.

Melt ⅓ cup butter in saucepan over low heat; add flour, stirring until smooth. Cook, stirring constantly, 1 minute. Gradually add 2½ cups milk; cook over medium heat, stirring constantly, until thickened and bubbly.

Stir in whipping cream and next 5 ingredients. Cook, stirring constantly, until cheese melts and mixture is smooth; stir in chicken, ham, and reserved mushrooms.

Add enough of remaining ½ cup milk for a thinner consistency, if desired. To serve, spoon into baked shells, and sprinkle with paprika.
Yield: 12 servings.

Note: Creamy Chicken-and-Ham Medley may be served over hot, cooked angel hair pasta instead of pastry. Sprinkle with freshly grated Parmesan cheese, if desired.

Shrimp-and-Chicken Casserole

1 (2½- to 3-pound) broiler-fryer
1 teaspoon salt
4 cups water
1 pound unpeeled, medium-size fresh shrimp
2 (16-ounce) packages frozen broccoli cuts, thawed and well drained
1 cup mayonnaise or salad dressing
1 (10¾-ounce) can cream of chicken soup, undiluted
1 (10¾-ounce) can cream of celery soup, undiluted
3 tablespoons lemon juice
¼ teaspoon white pepper
1 cup (4 ounces) shredded Cheddar cheese
½ cup soft breadcrumbs
1 tablespoon butter or margarine, melted
Paprika
Garnishes: shrimp and fresh parsley sprigs

Combine chicken and salt in a Dutch oven; add enough water to cover, and bring to a boil. Cover, reduce heat, and simmer 45 minutes or until chicken is tender. Drain; let chicken cool slightly. Bone chicken; cut into bite-size pieces, and set aside.

Bring 4 cups water to a boil; add shrimp, and cook 3 to 5 minutes. Drain; rinse with cold water. Peel and devein shrimp. Set 3 shrimp aside for garnish, if desired.

Spread broccoli evenly in a lightly greased 13- x 9- x 2-inch baking dish; set aside. Combine mayonnaise and next 4 ingredients; spread one-third over broccoli. Set aside remaining sauce.

Combine chicken and shrimp; spread evenly over casserole, and top with remaining sauce. Cover and chill up to 8 hours.

Remove casserole from refrigerator, and let stand at room temperature 30 minutes. Bake, covered, at 350° for 30 minutes. Uncover; sprinkle with cheese.

Combine breadcrumbs and butter; sprinkle over cheese. Bake 15 additional minutes or until casserole is hot and bubbly. Sprinkle with paprika. Garnish, if desired. **Yield: 10 servings.**

Note: Casserole may be assembled and baked immediately. Six chicken breast halves may be substituted for broiler-fryer.

Tipsy Chicken and Dressing

1 (8-ounce) package cornbread stuffing mix
2 large eggs
3 slices bread, crumbled
1 (14½-ounce) can chicken broth, undiluted
1 small onion, finely chopped
1 stalk celery, finely chopped
1 (14-ounce) can artichoke hearts, drained and quartered
8 skinned and boned chicken breast halves
8 (1-ounce) slices Swiss cheese
1 (10¾-ounce) can cream of celery soup, undiluted
1 cup white wine
½ teaspoon dried basil
4 mushrooms, sliced
¼ cup grated Parmesan cheese
2 tablespoons minced parsley
Garnish: fresh parsley sprigs

Combine first 6 ingredients; mix well. Divide mixture among 8 lightly greased individual 2-cup casserole dishes. Place 3 artichoke quarters in middle of dressing mixture; place chicken over artichokes. Top with Swiss cheese.

Combine soup, wine, and basil; pour over chicken. Top with mushrooms, Parmesan cheese, and minced parsley.

Cover and bake at 350° for 40 minutes. Uncover and bake 10 additional minutes. Garnish, if desired. **Yield: 8 servings.**

Creole Chicken and Grits

½ cup all-purpose flour
½ cup plus 3 tablespoons vegetable oil, divided
1 medium onion, chopped
1 medium-size green pepper, chopped
2 cloves garlic, minced
1 (10¾-ounce) can chicken broth, undiluted
1 (8-ounce) can tomato sauce
3 bay leaves
3 tablespoons all-purpose flour
1 teaspoon garlic salt
1 teaspoon ground red pepper
1 teaspoon dried oregano
1 teaspoon pepper
½ teaspoon dried thyme
2 pounds skinned and boned chicken breast
    halves, cut into bite-size pieces
Garlic-Cheese Grits

Combine ½ cup flour and ½ cup oil in a Dutch oven. Cook over medium-low heat, stirring constantly, 20 to 30 minutes or until roux is caramel-colored.

Add onion, green pepper, and garlic; cook, stirring constantly, 4 minutes. Add chicken broth, tomato sauce, and bay leaves. Cover, reduce heat, and simmer 20 minutes.

Combine 3 tablespoons flour and next 5 ingredients; dredge chicken in flour mixture.

Heat remaining 3 tablespoons oil in a large nonstick skillet over medium heat. Brown chicken on all sides in skillet in batches. Remove chicken from skillet; add to Dutch oven. Cover and simmer over low heat 5 minutes. Remove bay leaves. Serve over Garlic-Cheese Grits. **Yield: 8 servings.**

Garlic-Cheese Grits

7 cups water
1 teaspoon salt
2 cups quick-cooking grits, uncooked
2 (6-ounce) rolls process cheese food with garlic

Bring water to a boil in a Dutch oven; stir in salt and grits. Return mixture to a boil; reduce heat, and simmer 4 minutes, stirring occasionally. Add cheese, stirring until cheese melts.

Remove from heat. Press grits firmly into a greased 8-cup ring mold. Let stand 10 to 15 minutes. Unmold onto a serving plate. **Yield: 8 cups.**

Chicken Pilaf

½ cup all-purpose flour
1 teaspoon paprika
½ teaspoon salt
Dash of pepper
8 skinned and boned chicken breast halves
3 tablespoons butter or margarine
2 cups boiling water
2 chicken-flavored bouillon cubes
4 medium carrots, diced
1 medium onion, chopped
1 cup uncooked regular rice
½ teaspoon dried thyme

Combine first 4 ingredients. Cut each chicken breast half in half lengthwise; dredge in flour mixture.

Melt butter over medium heat in a large, heavy ovenproof skillet; add chicken, and brown on both sides. Remove chicken from skillet, and set aside. Reserve drippings in skillet.

Combine boiling water and bouillon cubes, stirring until bouillon dissolves.

Cook carrot and onion in reserved drippings in skillet until tender. Add rice; cook over low heat until lightly browned. Add bouillon mixture and thyme, stirring well. Arrange chicken over rice mixture.

Cover and bake at 350° for 1 hour. **Yield: 8 servings.**

Country Captain Chicken

Country Captain Chicken

½ cup all-purpose flour
1 teaspoon salt
½ teaspoon pepper
1 (2½- to 3-pound) broiler-fryer, cut up
Vegetable oil
2 medium onions, chopped
2 medium-size green peppers, chopped
¼ cup chopped celery
1 clove garlic, minced
2 (16-ounce) cans whole tomatoes, undrained
    and chopped
¼ cup currants
2 teaspoons curry powder
¾ teaspoon salt
½ teaspoon ground white pepper
½ teaspoon ground thyme
3 cups hot cooked rice
1½ tablespoons minced fresh parsley
3 tablespoons cornstarch
¼ cup cold water
¼ cup sliced natural almonds, toasted

Combine first 3 ingredients; stir well. Dredge chicken in flour mixture.

Pour oil to a depth of ½ inch into a large heavy skillet. Fry chicken in hot oil (350°) until browned.

Arrange chicken in a 13- x 9- x 2-inch baking dish; set aside. Drain pan drippings, reserving 2 tablespoons drippings in skillet.

Cook onion, green pepper, celery, and garlic in pan drippings until vegetables are tender. Add tomatoes and next 5 ingredients; stir well. Spoon sauce over chicken in baking dish.

Cover and bake at 350° for 40 to 50 minutes or until chicken is tender.

Transfer chicken to a large serving platter with a slotted spoon, reserving sauce in baking dish. Combine rice and parsley, tossing gently to combine; spoon around chicken. Set aside, and keep warm.

Transfer sauce to a medium saucepan. Combine cornstarch and water, stirring until smooth; stir into sauce. Bring sauce to a boil; cook, stirring constantly, 1 minute or until slightly thickened. Spoon sauce over chicken. Sprinkle almonds over chicken. Serve immediately. **Yield: 4 servings.**

Chicken-Wild Rice Casserole

1 (6-ounce) package long grain and wild rice
¼ cup butter or margarine
¼ cup all-purpose flour
½ teaspoon salt
¼ teaspoon pepper
1 (13-ounce) can evaporated milk
½ cup chicken broth
2½ cups chopped cooked chicken
1 (3-ounce) can sliced mushrooms, drained
1 (14-ounce) can artichoke hearts, drained
    and chopped
¼ cup chopped pimiento (optional)
¼ cup slivered almonds, lightly toasted

Prepare rice according to package directions; set aside.

Melt butter in a heavy saucepan over low heat; add flour, salt, and pepper, stirring until smooth. Cook, stirring constantly, 1 minute. Gradually add milk and broth; cook over medium heat, stirring constantly, until thickened and bubbly.

Combine sauce, rice, chicken, mushrooms, artichokes, and, if desired, pimiento. Spoon into a lightly greased 2-quart casserole. Sprinkle with almonds.

Bake, uncovered, at 350° for 30 to 35 minutes or until thoroughly heated. **Yield: 6 servings.**

Note: To make ahead, prepare as directed above, but do not bake. Cover and refrigerate up to 8 hours. Let stand, covered, at room temperature 30 minutes. Uncover and bake as directed.

Chicken Curry

6 skinned chicken breast halves
2 cloves garlic
2 bay leaves
4 whole peppercorns
1 teaspoon salt
1 carrot, sliced
1 onion, sliced
½ cup chopped celery
1 apple, peeled, cored, and chopped
3 tablespoons butter or margarine, melted
1½ tablespoons curry powder
½ teaspoon chili powder
3 tablespoons all-purpose flour
¼ teaspoon ground mace
¼ teaspoon ground allspice
¼ teaspoon ground nutmeg
¼ teaspoon ground cinnamon
¼ teaspoon ground cloves
Hot cooked rice
Condiments: flaked coconut, chopped peanuts,
    chopped green onions, chutney, raisins,
    cooked and crumbled bacon
Garnish: celery leaves

Combine first 5 ingredients in a Dutch oven; add water to cover. Bring to a boil over medium heat; cover, reduce heat, and simmer 35 to 40 minutes or until chicken is tender. Drain; discard peppercorns, bay leaves, and garlic. Reserve 2 cups broth. Bone chicken; cut into bite-size pieces.

Cook carrot and next 3 ingredients in butter in a Dutch oven over medium heat, stirring constantly, 10 minutes or until tender. Add curry powder and chili powder, and cook 5 minutes, stirring occasionally.

Stir in ¾ cup reserved broth. Place apple mixture in container of an electric blender, and process until smooth. Add flour, and process until well blended.

Return mixture to Dutch oven, and cook until thickened. Gradually add 1¼ cups reserved chicken broth and cook, stirring constantly, 5 minutes.

Add mace and next 4 ingredients; gently stir in chicken.

Serve over rice with assorted condiments. Garnish, if desired. **Yield: 6 servings.**

Ginger-Nut Chicken

1 tablespoon butter or margarine
2 skinned and boned chicken breast halves
1½ cups broccoli flowerets
½ cup green onions, cut into 1-inch pieces
½ cup celery, cut into 1-inch pieces
3 (⅛-inch) slices fresh gingerroot
2 tablespoons cornstarch
½ cup water, divided
1 tablespoon soy sauce
¼ teaspoon lemon-pepper seasoning
⅛ teaspoon garlic salt
⅓ cup dry roasted peanuts
Hot cooked rice

Place butter in a 1½-quart casserole. Microwave at HIGH 45 seconds or until melted.

Cut chicken into bite-size pieces. Add to casserole, and coat with butter. Cover and microwave at HIGH 4 minutes, stirring after 2 minutes.

Add broccoli and next 3 ingredients. Microwave at HIGH 2 minutes.

Combine cornstarch and ¼ cup water in a glass measuring cup, stirring well. Add remaining ¼ cup water, soy sauce, lemon-pepper seasoning, and garlic salt; stir well. Pour cornstarch mixture over chicken and vegetables.

Cover and microwave at HIGH 2 to 3 minutes or until sauce is slightly thickened; stir once. Stir in peanuts. Remove ginger, and serve over rice. **Yield: 2 to 3 servings.**

Ginger-Nut Chicken

Chicken Cacciatore

¼ cup all-purpose flour
½ teaspoon salt
½ teaspoon pepper
8 skinned and boned chicken breast halves
¼ cup olive oil
1 large onion, chopped
3 or 4 cloves garlic, minced
½ pound fresh mushrooms, sliced
2 (16-ounce) cans whole tomatoes, undrained and quartered
1 (4-ounce) jar whole pimientos, undrained and sliced
3 bay leaves
½ cup sweet vermouth
1 teaspoon dried thyme
1 teaspoon dried oregano
½ teaspoon salt
¼ teaspoon pepper
2 medium-size green peppers, seeded and cut into strips
Hot cooked spaghetti

Combine first 3 ingredients; dredge chicken in flour mixture. Brown chicken in hot oil in a Dutch oven over medium-high heat. Remove chicken from Dutch oven, reserving drippings; drain chicken on paper towels.

Cook onion and garlic in drippings in Dutch oven over medium heat 5 minutes. Stir in mushrooms and next 8 ingredients. Add chicken to mixture in Dutch oven. Bring to a boil; reduce heat, and simmer, uncovered, 30 minutes, stirring occasionally. Stir in green pepper; cook, uncovered, 30 minutes, stirring occasionally. Remove and discard bay leaves. Serve over spaghetti.
Yield: 8 servings.

Note: "Cacciatore" means hunter's style in Italian. Served with generous amounts of spaghetti, this classic dish always includes tomatoes, mushrooms, onions, and herbs.

Chicken Fettuccine Supreme

¼ cup butter or margarine
1¼ pounds skinned and boned chicken breast halves, cut into ¾-inch pieces
3 cups sliced fresh mushrooms
1 cup chopped green onions
1 small sweet red pepper, cut into thin strips
1 clove garlic, crushed
½ teaspoon salt
½ teaspoon pepper
10 ounces uncooked fettuccine
¾ cup half-and-half
½ cup butter or margarine, melted
¼ cup chopped fresh parsley
¼ teaspoon salt
¼ teaspoon pepper
½ cup grated Parmesan cheese
1 cup chopped pecans, toasted

Melt ¼ cup butter in a large skillet over medium heat; add chicken, and cook, stirring constantly, until browned. Remove chicken from skillet, reserving pan drippings in skillet; set chicken aside.

Add mushrooms and next 5 ingredients to pan drippings in skillet, and cook, stirring constantly, until vegetables are tender.

Add chicken; reduce heat, and cook 15 minutes or until chicken is tender and mixture is thoroughly heated. Set aside, and keep warm.

Cook fettuccine according to package directions, omitting salt; drain. Place fettuccine in a large bowl.

Combine half-and-half and next 4 ingredients in a small bowl; stir well. Add to fettuccine; toss gently to combine.

Add chicken mixture and Parmesan cheese to fettuccine; toss gently to combine. Sprinkle with pecans, and serve immediately. **Yield: 6 servings.**

Chicken Fettuccine Supreme

Creamy Chicken Tetrazzini

Creamy Chicken Tetrazzini

1 (3- to 4-pound) broiler-fryer
1 teaspoon salt
1 teaspoon pepper
1 (8-ounce) package spaghetti
1 large green pepper, chopped
1 cup sliced fresh mushrooms
1 small onion, chopped
¼ cup butter or margarine, melted
¼ cup all-purpose flour
½ teaspoon salt
½ teaspoon garlic powder
½ teaspoon poultry seasoning
½ teaspoon pepper
1 cup half-and-half
2 cups (8 ounces) shredded sharp Cheddar
   cheese, divided
1 (10¾-ounce) can cream of mushroom soup,
   undiluted
¾ cup grated Parmesan cheese, divided
¼ cup sherry
1 (4-ounce) jar sliced pimiento, drained
1 teaspoon paprika
¾ cup sliced almonds, toasted

Combine first 3 ingredients in a Dutch oven; add water to cover. Bring to a boil. Cover, reduce heat, and simmer 45 minutes or until chicken is tender. Remove chicken from broth, reserving broth.

Let chicken cool slightly. Bone and coarsely shred chicken; set aside.

Add enough water to reserved broth to measure 3 quarts; bring to a boil. Cook spaghetti in broth according to package directions. Drain and set aside.

Cook green pepper, mushrooms, and onion in butter in a Dutch oven over medium heat, stirring constantly, until tender. Add flour and next 4 ingredients; stir until smooth. Cook, stirring constantly 1 minute. Gradually stir in half-and-half, and cook until thickened, stirring gently.

Add ¾ cup Cheddar cheese, stirring until cheese melts. Add chicken, mushroom soup, ½ cup Parmesan cheese, sherry, and pimiento; stir well.

Combine chicken mixture and cooked spaghetti, tossing gently until thoroughly combined. Spoon into a greased 13- x 9- x 2-inch baking dish.

Bake, uncovered, at 350° for 20 to 25 minutes or until thoroughly heated.

Combine remaining ¼ cup Parmesan cheese and paprika; stir well. Sprinkle remaining 1¼ cups Cheddar cheese in diagonal rows across top of casserole. Repeat procedure with almonds and Parmesan-paprika mixture. Bake 5 additional minutes or until Cheddar cheese melts. **Yield: 6 to 8 servings.**

Chicken Manicotti

8 manicotti shells
1 (10¾-ounce) can creamy chicken mushroom
   soup, undiluted
½ cup sour cream
2 cups chopped cooked chicken
¼ cup chopped onion
2 tablespoons butter or margarine, melted
1 (4-ounce) can sliced mushrooms, undrained
1 cup (4 ounces) shredded Cheddar or
   Monterey Jack cheese

Cook manicotti shells according to package directions, omitting salt; drain and set aside.

Combine soup and sour cream; stir well. Combine half of soup mixture and chicken; stir well. Set aside remaining soup mixture. Stuff manicotti shells with chicken mixture; place in a greased 11- x 7- x 1½-inch baking dish.

Cook onion in butter over medium heat in a large skillet, stirring constantly, until tender; add mushrooms and reserved soup mixture. Spoon over manicotti.

Bake, uncovered, at 350° for 15 minutes. Sprinkle with cheese, and bake 5 additional minutes. **Yield: 4 servings.**

Cheesy Chicken Spaghetti

1 (6-pound) hen
1 (10-ounce) package spaghetti
1½ cups chopped onion
1 cup chopped green pepper
1 cup chopped celery
1 (4-ounce) jar diced pimiento, drained
1 (6-ounce) jar sliced mushrooms, drained
1 (16-ounce) loaf process American cheese,
    cubed
½ teaspoon salt
½ teaspoon pepper

Place hen in a Dutch oven; add water to cover. Bring to a boil; cover, reduce heat, and simmer 1½ hours or until tender.

Remove hen, reserving 6 cups broth; let hen cool slightly. Bone, and cut into bite-size pieces; set aside.

Bring 1 quart reserved broth to a boil in Dutch oven; gradually add spaghetti. Cook, uncovered, over medium heat 10 to 13 minutes. Do not drain.

Combine onion, green pepper, celery, and remaining 2 cups reserved broth in a medium saucepan. Bring to a boil; reduce heat and simmer 10 minutes or until vegetables are tender. Drain.

Add chicken, cooked vegetables, pimiento, and mushrooms to spaghetti, stirring well. Add cheese cubes, salt, and pepper, stirring until cheese melts. **Yield: 8 servings.**

Extra Chicken Broth?

• Fresh broth can be refrigerated 3 to 4 days.
• Freeze broth in a variety of containers or try ice-cube trays. Transfer the cubes to a plastic bag once frozen. Each cube yields about 2 tablespoons of broth.

Chicken Lasagna

1 (2½- to 3-pound) broiler-fryer
6 cups water
1 teaspoon salt
1 clove garlic, minced
2 tablespoons butter, melted
1 (10¾-ounce) can cream of celery soup,
    undiluted
½ teaspoon dried oregano
¼ teaspoon pepper
8 lasagna noodles, uncooked
1 (8-ounce) loaf process American cheese, cut
    in ¼-inch slices, divided
2 cups (8 ounces) shredded mozzarella
    cheese, divided
2 tablespoons grated Parmesan cheese

Combine first 3 ingredients in a Dutch oven; bring to a boil. Cover, reduce heat, and simmer 45 minutes or until chicken is tender.

Drain, reserving broth, and let cool slightly. Bone chicken and cut into bite-size pieces; set aside.

Cook garlic in butter in a skillet over medium-high heat, stirring constantly, 2 minutes. Add celery soup, ¾ cup reserved chicken broth, oregano, and pepper.

Cook lasagna noodles according to package directions in remaining reserved chicken broth, adding more water, if necessary; drain.

Spoon a small amount of sauce into a lightly greased 11- x 7- x 1½-inch baking dish. Layer with half each of lasagna noodles, sauce, chicken, and American and mozzarella cheeses. Repeat procedure with noodles, sauce, and chicken, reserving remaining cheeses to add later.

Bake at 350° for 25 minutes; top with remaining cheeses, and bake 5 additional minutes. Let stand 10 minutes. **Yield: 6 servings.**

Note: To save time, cook chicken in a pressure cooker; follow manufacturer's instructions.

From the Skillet & Wok

These recipes prove that there's more than one way to fry chicken.
Choose from pan-fried, deep-fried, and stir-fried favorites.

Crispy Fried Chicken, Spicy Fried Chicken, Italian Chicken Cutlets

Fried Cheese-Stuffed Chicken Thighs, Chicken Kiev, Cashew-Chicken Stir-Fry

Italian-Seasoned Fried Chicken, Chicken Piccata, Bourbon Chicken with Gravy

Chicken Scaloppine with Lemon Sauce, Crispy Chicken Croquettes

Chicken-in-a-Garden (page 111)

Crispy Fried Chicken

Crispy Fried Chicken

1 (3- to 3½-pound) broiler-fryer, cut up
½ teaspoon salt
⅛ teaspoon black pepper
1½ cups all-purpose flour
1 teaspoon salt
¾ teaspoon black pepper
½ teaspoon ground red pepper
¼ teaspoon paprika
1 large egg, beaten
½ cup buttermilk
Vegetable oil

Season chicken with ½ teaspoon salt and ⅛ teaspoon black pepper; set aside.

Combine flour and next 4 ingredients; stir well, and set aside. Combine egg and buttermilk; stir well.

Dip chicken in egg mixture; dredge in flour mixture, coating each piece well. Repeat procedure, heavily coating chicken pieces.

Pour oil to depth of 1 inch into a large heavy skillet; heat to 350°. Fry chicken 20 to 25 minutes or until golden, turning to brown both sides. Drain well on paper towels. **Yield: 4 servings.**

Spicy Fried Chicken

6 skinned and boned chicken breast halves
2 cups water
2 tablespoons hot sauce
1 cup self-rising flour
1 teaspoon garlic salt
½ teaspoon pepper
1 teaspoon paprika
1 teaspoon red pepper
Vegetable oil

Place chicken in a shallow dish or heavy-duty, zip-top plastic bag. Combine water and hot sauce; pour over chicken. Cover or seal, and marinate 1 hour in refrigerator, turning once.

Combine flour and next 4 ingredients. Remove chicken from marinade, and dredge in flour mixture, coating well.

Pour oil to depth of 1 inch into a heavy skillet; heat to 350°. Fry chicken 5 to 6 minutes on each side or until golden brown. Drain well on paper towels. **Yield: 6 servings.**

Italian-Seasoned Fried Chicken

¾ cup Italian-seasoned breadcrumbs
½ cup grated Parmesan cheese
¼ cup minced fresh parsley
¾ teaspoon dried oregano
1 large egg, beaten
½ cup milk
1 tablespoon all-purpose flour
1 (3- to 3½-pound) broiler-fryer, cut up
Vegetable oil

Combine first 4 ingredients; stir well, and set aside. Combine egg, milk, and flour; stir well. Dip chicken in egg mixture; dredge in breadcrumb mixture, coating well.

Pour oil to depth of 1 inch into a large, heavy skillet; heat to 350°. Fry chicken 20 to 25 minutes or until golden, turning to brown both sides. Drain well on paper towels. **Yield: 4 servings.**

Fried Chicken Technique

Fry chicken pieces in 1 inch of hot oil until golden, turning with tongs to brown both sides evenly.

Italian Chicken Cutlets

(pictured on page 2)

6 skinned and boned chicken breast halves
1 cup Italian-seasoned breadcrumbs
½ cup freshly grated Romano or Parmesan
    cheese
¼ cup all-purpose flour
1 (0.8-ounce) envelope light Italian salad
    dressing mix
2 teaspoons dried oregano
¼ teaspoon garlic powder
2 large eggs, beaten
⅓ cup vegetable oil
Garnish: green onion strips

Place chicken between 2 sheets of heavy-duty plastic wrap; flatten to ¼-inch thickness, using a meat mallet or rolling pin.

Combine breadcrumbs and next 5 ingredients; dip chicken in eggs, and dredge in breadcrumbs.

Heat oil in a large skillet over medium heat. Add chicken, and cook 3 to 4 minutes on each side or until golden brown, adding extra oil if necessary. Drain on paper towels. Garnish, if desired. **Yield: 6 servings.**

Chicken Piccata

6 skinned and boned chicken breast halves
⅓ cup all-purpose flour
1 teaspoon salt
¼ teaspoon pepper
¼ cup butter or margarine
¼ cup lemon juice
1 lemon, thinly sliced
2 tablespoons chopped fresh parsley

Place chicken between 2 sheets of heavy-duty plastic wrap; flatten to ¼-inch thickness, using a meat mallet or rolling pin.

Combine flour, salt, and pepper; dredge chicken in flour mixture.

Melt butter in a large skillet over medium heat. Add chicken, and cook 3 to 4 minutes on each side or until golden brown. Remove chicken, and drain on paper towels; keep warm.

Add lemon juice and lemon slices to pan drippings in skillet; cook until thoroughly heated. Pour lemon mixture over chicken; sprinkle with parsley. **Yield: 6 servings.**

Chicken Scaloppine with Lemon Sauce

6 skinned and boned chicken breast halves,
    halved
1 cup all-purpose flour
¼ teaspoon pepper
2 large eggs, beaten
¼ cup butter or margarine
¼ cup vegetable oil
½ to ¾ pound fresh mushrooms, thinly sliced
¼ cup water
½ cup Chablis or other dry white wine
½ cup lemon juice
½ cup chopped fresh parsley

Place chicken between 2 sheets of heavy-duty plastic wrap; flatten to ¼-inch thickness, using a meat mallet or rolling pin.

Combine flour and pepper; dip chicken in egg, and dredge in flour mixture.

Heat butter and oil in a heavy skillet; cook chicken in skillet over medium heat about 4 minutes on each side or until golden brown. Place chicken on a serving platter; keep warm.

Add mushrooms and water to pan drippings; cook over medium heat, stirring often, about 3 minutes. Spoon mushrooms over chicken.

Add wine and lemon juice to skillet; heat thoroughly. Pour sauce over chicken; sprinkle with parsley. **Yield: 6 servings.**

Bourbon Chicken with Gravy

¼ cup butter or margarine
4 pounds skinned chicken pieces
¾ cup bourbon, divided
1 medium onion, finely chopped
2 tablespoons dried parsley flakes
1 teaspoon dried thyme
½ teaspoon salt
⅛ teaspoon pepper
¼ cup whipping cream

Melt butter in a large, heavy skillet over medium heat; add chicken, and brown on both sides. Add ¼ cup bourbon. Carefully ignite bourbon with a long match, and let burn until flames die.

Add onion and next 4 ingredients. Stir in remaining ½ cup bourbon, stirring until blended. Bring to a boil; cover, reduce heat, and simmer 30 minutes or until chicken is tender. Place on a serving plate, reserving liquid in skillet.

Add whipping cream to skillet; bring to a boil, stirring constantly. Cook over medium heat until thickened. Serve with chicken. **Yield: 6 servings.**

Sautéed Chicken Livers

1 pound chicken livers
⅓ cup Chablis or other dry white wine
2½ tablespoons lemon juice
¼ teaspoon salt
¼ teaspoon pepper
½ to ¾ cup all-purpose flour
3 to 4 tablespoons vegetable oil

Cut chicken livers in half. Combine wine and lemon juice in a shallow dish; add livers and toss. Cover and marinate in refrigerator 30 minutes.

Drain livers. Sprinkle with salt and pepper; dredge in flour. Cook in hot oil about 5 minutes or until done. Drain well, and serve immediately. **Yield: 4 servings.**

Chicken Cutlet Shortcuts

• Save time by buying skinned and boned chicken breasts.
• Save money by pounding these breasts into convenient cutlets. Place chicken breasts between 2 sheets of heavy-duty plastic wrap. Starting at the center and working outward, gently pound chicken to desired thickness with the flat side of a meat mallet.

Fried Cheese-Stuffed Chicken Thighs

8 skinned and boned chicken thighs
½ (8-ounce) package Swiss cheese
8 slices bacon, partially cooked
2 egg whites, slightly beaten
1½ tablespoons lemon juice
¾ cup all-purpose flour
1½ teaspoons lemon-pepper seasoning
Vegetable oil

Place chicken between 2 sheets of heavy-duty plastic wrap; flatten to ¼-inch thickness, using a meat mallet or rolling pin.

Slice cheese lengthwise to make 8 even strips. Place 1 strip of cheese in center of each chicken thigh. Fold long sides of chicken over cheese; fold ends of chicken over, and wrap each with a slice of bacon. Secure with wooden picks.

Combine egg white and lemon juice; combine flour and lemon-pepper seasoning. Dip chicken in egg mixture; dredge in flour mixture.

Pour oil to depth of 1 inch into a heavy skillet; heat to 350°. Fry chicken 15 minutes or until golden, turning once. Drain on paper towels. **Yield: 8 servings.**

Crispy Chicken Croquettes

2 tablespoons chopped onion
1 tablespoon butter or margarine, melted
1 tablespoon all-purpose flour
¾ cup water
1¼ teaspoons chicken-flavored bouillon granules
½ teaspoon dry mustard
½ teaspoon pepper
4 cups finely chopped cooked chicken
1 large egg, beaten
3 tablespoons dry white wine
1 cup round buttery cracker crumbs
Vegetable oil
Peppery Cream Sauce

Cook onion in butter in a large saucepan until tender. Add flour, stirring until smooth. Cook, stirring constantly, 1 minute. Gradually add water; cook over medium heat, stirring constantly, until sauce is thickened and bubbly.

Stir in bouillon granules and next 5 ingredients. Cook over medium heat, stirring constantly, 3 to 5 minutes. Remove from heat; cover and chill.

Shape mixture into croquettes, and roll in cracker crumbs. Pour oil to depth of 2 to 3 inches into a Dutch oven; heat to 350°. Fry croquettes until golden brown. Drain on paper towels. Serve with Peppery Cream Sauce. **Yield: 10 croquettes.**

Peppery Cream Sauce

3 tablespoons butter or margarine
3 tablespoons all-purpose flour
1½ cups milk
½ teaspoon salt
½ teaspoon pepper

Melt butter in a heavy saucepan over low heat; add flour, stirring until smooth. Cook, stirring constantly, 1 minute. Gradually add milk; cook over medium heat, stirring constantly, until sauce is thickened and bubbly. Stir in salt and pepper. **Yield: 1½ cups.**

Chicken Kiev

¼ cup plus 2 tablespoons butter, softened
1 tablespoon chopped fresh parsley
1 small clove garlic, minced
¼ teaspoon dried tarragon
¼ teaspoon salt
⅛ teaspoon ground white pepper
6 skinned and boned chicken breast halves
1 large egg, beaten
1 tablespoon water
½ cup all-purpose flour
1½ to 2 cups soft breadcrumbs
Vegetable oil

Combine first 6 ingredients in a small bowl; stir until blended. Shape butter mixture into a 3-inch stick; cover and freeze about 45 minutes or until firm.

Place chicken between 2 sheets of heavy-duty plastic wrap; flatten to ¼-inch thickness, using a meat mallet or rolling pin.

Cut butter into 6 pats; place one pat in center of each chicken breast. Fold long sides of chicken over butter; fold ends over, and secure with wooden picks.

Combine egg and water, beating well. Dredge chicken in flour; dip in egg mixture, and dredge in breadcrumbs.

Pour oil to depth of 2 to 3 inches into a Dutch oven; heat to 350°. Fry chicken 3 to 4 minutes on each side or until browned. Drain well on paper towels. **Yield: 6 servings.**

Chicken Kiev

Considered an elegant entrée, this famous Russian dish is worth the effort. Take care when cutting into Chicken Kiev as the traditional herbed butter may spurt out.

Chicken Kiev

Cashew-Chicken Stir-Fry

1½ **pounds skinned and boned chicken breast halves**
½ **cup Chablis or other dry white wine**
½ **cup teriyaki sauce**
1 **tablespoon grated fresh gingerroot**
1 **clove garlic, crushed**
2 **tablespoons vegetable oil, divided**
1 **cup diagonally sliced celery**
½ **cup sliced green onions**
2 **tablespoons soy sauce**
1 **tablespoon plus 1 teaspoon cornstarch**
2 **teaspoons brown sugar**
2 **teaspoons chicken-flavored bouillon granules**
1¼ **cups boiling water**
½ **cup roasted cashews**
Chow mein noodles

Cut chicken lengthwise into thin strips; place in a large shallow dish. Combine wine, teriyaki sauce, gingerroot, and garlic; stir well. Pour marinade mixture over chicken; toss gently to coat. Cover and marinate in refrigerator at least 2 hours. Drain chicken, discarding marinade.

Pour 1 tablespoon oil around top of preheated wok, coating sides; heat at medium-high (350°) for 2 minutes. Add celery and green onions, and stir-fry 2 to 3 minutes or until vegetables are crisp-tender. Remove vegetables from wok, and set aside.

Add remaining 1 tablespoon oil to wok. Add chicken, and stir-fry 3 to 4 minutes or until chicken is done. Remove chicken from wok, and set aside.

Combine soy sauce, cornstarch, and brown sugar in a small bowl, stirring well. Dissolve bouillon granules in boiling water; add cornstarch mixture, stirring well. Add to wok; cook, stirring gently, until mixture is thickened.

Add reserved vegetables, chicken, and cashews to wok; stir-fry 30 seconds or until thoroughly heated. Serve over chow mein noodles.
Yield: 6 servings.

Cashew-Chicken Stir-Fry Techniques

Cut chicken lengthwise into thin strips; marinate in refrigerator at least 2 hours.

Stir-fry celery and green onions in hot oil in a wok 2 to 3 minutes or until crisp-tender.

Dissolve bouillon granules in boiling water; add cornstarch mixture and stir well.

Cashew-Chicken Stir-Fry

Szechuan Chicken with Cashews

1 pound skinned and boned chicken breast
   halves
2 tablespoons soy sauce
1 teaspoon sherry
2 tablespoons water
1 tablespoon cornstarch
3 tablespoons vegetable oil
2 dried whole red peppers
2 tablespoons chopped fresh gingerroot
2 tablespoons soy sauce
1 tablespoon sherry
¼ cup plus 1 tablespoon water
1 tablespoon cornstarch
1 tablespoon sugar
1 teaspoon coarsely ground black pepper
2 teaspoons white vinegar
1 teaspoon vegetable oil
½ cup coarsely chopped fresh mushrooms
1 green pepper, cut into thin strips
4 green onions, cut into ½-inch pieces
2 stalks celery, diagonally sliced
1 cup cashews
Hot cooked rice

Place chicken between 2 sheets of heavy-duty plastic wrap; flatten to ¼-inch thickness, using a meat mallet or rolling pin. Cut chicken into bite-size pieces.

Combine 2 tablespoons soy sauce and next 3 ingredients in a medium bowl; mix well. Add chicken; cover and refrigerate 20 minutes.

Pour 3 tablespoons oil around top of preheated wok, coating sides; heat at medium high (350°) for 2 minutes. Add red peppers; stir-fry 1 minute and discard. Add gingerroot to hot oil; stir-fry 1 minute and discard.

Combine 2 tablespoons soy sauce and next 7 ingredients; mix well, and set aside.

Add chicken, mushrooms, green pepper, green onions, and celery. Stir-fry about 5 minutes or until vegetables are crisp-tender.

Pour reserved soy sauce mixture over chicken mixture; add cashews and cook, stirring constantly, until thickened. Serve over hot cooked rice. **Yield: 4 servings.**

Princess Chicken

2 tablespoons cornstarch
2 tablespoons soy sauce
1 pound skinned and boned chicken breast
    halves, cut into 1-inch pieces
2 tablespoons soy sauce
1 tablespoon sugar
1 tablespoon rice wine or white wine
1 teaspoon cornstarch
1 teaspoon sesame oil
¼ cup peanut or vegetable oil
5 or 6 dried whole red peppers
2 teaspoons grated fresh gingerroot
½ cup chopped roasted peanuts

Combine 2 tablespoons cornstarch and 2 tablespoons soy sauce in a medium bowl; stir well. Add chicken, mixing well. Cover and refrigerate 30 minutes.

Combine 2 tablespoons soy sauce and next 4 ingredients; mix well, and set aside.

Pour peanut oil around top of preheated wok, coating sides; heat at medium-high (350°) for 1 minute. Add chicken, and stir-fry 2 minutes. Remove and drain on paper towels.

Reserve 2 tablespoons drippings in wok. Heat at medium-high (350°) for 30 seconds. Add red peppers, and stir-fry until dark brown. Add gingerroot and chicken; stir-fry 1 minute. Add wine mixture. Cook until slightly thickened. Stir in peanuts. **Yield: 4 servings.**

Lemon Chicken and Vegetables

3 tablespoons vegetable oil, divided
4 skinned and boned chicken breast halves,
   cut into ½-inch strips
1 lemon, sliced
½ cup sliced celery
½ medium onion, sliced
1 cup sliced yellow squash or zucchini
½ cup sliced mushrooms
½ cup sweet red pepper strips
½ cup frozen English peas, thawed
½ cup fresh snow pea pods
1 teaspoon pepper
1 tablespoon lemon juice

Heat 1½ tablespoons oil to medium-high (350°) in a large skillet. Add chicken and lemon slices, and stir-fry 2 minutes or until lightly browned. Remove from skillet. Set aside.

Heat remaining 1½ tablespoons oil to medium-high in skillet. Add celery and next 4 ingredients; stir-fry 2 minutes or until vegetables are crisp-tender.

Add chicken, peas, and remaining ingredients to skillet. Stir-fry on medium-high until thoroughly heated. Serve immediately. **Yield: 4 servings.**

Orange Chicken Stir-Fry

3 tablespoons vegetable oil
6 skinned and boned chicken breast halves,
   cut into 1-inch pieces
2 tablespoons grated orange rind
1 teaspoon freshly grated gingerroot
¼ teaspoon hot sauce
4 green onions, cut into ¼-inch slices
1 cup orange juice
⅓ cup soy sauce
¼ cup sugar
1½ tablespoons cornstarch
2 oranges, peeled, seeded, and sectioned
Hot cooked rice

Pour oil around top of preheated wok, coating sides; heat at medium-high (350°) for 2 minutes. Add chicken and stir-fry 2 minutes or until lightly browned. Remove from wok, and drain well on paper towels.

Add orange rind, gingerroot, and hot sauce to wok; stir-fry 1½ minutes.

Return chicken to wok; stir-fry 3 minutes.

Combine green onions, orange juice, and next 3 ingredients; mix well. Add orange juice mixture and orange sections to wok; stir-fry 3 minutes or until thickened. Serve over rice. **Yield: 6 servings.**

Chicken-Vegetable Stir-Fry

½ cup soy sauce
¼ cup vegetable oil or sesame seed oil
2 teaspoons sesame seeds
6 skinned and boned chicken breast halves
2 cups broccoli flowerets
1 onion, thinly sliced and separated into rings
½ pound fresh snow pea pods
½ cup thinly sliced celery
½ cup sliced fresh mushrooms
1 tablespoon cornstarch
½ cup water
Hot cooked brown rice

Combine first 3 ingredients in a medium bowl, stirring well; set aside. Cut chicken into 2-inch strips, and add to marinade, mixing well. Cover and refrigerate at least 30 minutes.

Preheat wok to medium-high (350°). Add chicken mixture, and stir-fry 2 to 3 minutes. Remove chicken from wok, and set aside.

Add broccoli and onion to wok; stir-fry 2 minutes. Add snow peas, celery, and mushrooms; stir-fry 2 minutes or until vegetables are crisp-tender. Add chicken to wok.

Combine cornstarch and water; add to wok. Cook, stirring constantly, until thickened. Serve over brown rice. **Yield: 6 servings.**

Chicken Chinese

Chicken Chinese

2 skinned and boned chicken breast halves,
   cut into thin strips
2 cloves garlic, minced
½ teaspoon peeled, grated gingerroot
2 tablespoons peanut oil, divided
1 sweet red pepper, cut into thin strips
1 medium onion, cut into thin strips
1 cup broccoli flowerets
1 (13¾-ounce) can ready-to-serve, fat-free,
   reduced-sodium chicken broth
1½ tablespoons cornstarch
2 tablespoons commercial plum sauce
1 tablespoon Worcestershire sauce
1 tablespoon soy sauce
Chow mein noodles

Combine chicken strips, garlic, and ginger-root; toss gently. Cover and chill in refrigerator 30 minutes.

Pour 1 tablespoon peanut oil around top of a preheated wok, coating sides; heat at medium-high (350°) for 1 minute. Add chicken; stir-fry 3 minutes. Remove chicken from wok; set aside.

Pour remaining 1 tablespoon peanut oil into wok. Add red pepper, onion, and broccoli; stir-fry 2 minutes. Remove from wok; set aside.

Combine chicken broth and next 4 ingredients, stirring until smooth; add to wok. Bring to a boil, stirring constantly, for 1 minute. Add chicken and vegetables; cook until thoroughly heated. Serve with noodles. **Yield: 2 servings.**

Chicken-in-a-Garden

(pictured on page 99)

3 tablespoons peanut or vegetable oil, divided
2 tablespoons soy sauce, divided
1½ teaspoons cornstarch
½ teaspoon garlic powder
¼ teaspoon pepper
6 skinned and boned chicken breast halves,
    cut into 1-inch pieces
3 green peppers, cut into 1-inch pieces
1 cup diagonally sliced celery (1-inch pieces)
8 scallions, cut into ½-inch slices
1 (6-ounce) package frozen snow pea pods,
    thawed and drained
2½ tablespoons cornstarch
¾ cup water
¾ teaspoon chicken-flavored bouillon granules
⅛ teaspoon ground ginger
3 medium tomatoes, peeled and cut into eighths
Hot cooked rice

Combine 1 tablespoon oil, 1 tablespoon soy
sauce, 1½ teaspoons cornstarch, garlic powder,
and pepper in a medium bowl; stir well. Add
chicken; cover and refrigerate 20 minutes.

Pour remaining 2 tablespoons oil around top
of preheated wok, coating sides; heat at medium-
high (350°) for 2 minutes. Add green pepper, and
stir-fry 4 minutes. Add celery, scallions, and
snow peas; stir-fry 2 minutes. Remove vegetables
from wok, and set aside.

Combine remaining 1 tablespoon soy sauce and
2½ tablespoons cornstarch; stir in water, bouillon
granules, and ginger. Set mixture aside.

Add chicken to wok, and stir-fry 3 minutes;
add stir-fried vegetables, tomato, and bouillon
mixture. Stir-fry over low heat (225°) for 3 minutes
or until thickened and bubbly. Serve over rice.
Yield: 6 servings.

Sweet-and-Sour Chicken

1 (20-ounce) can pineapple chunks, undrained
¼ cup cider vinegar
3 tablespoons soy sauce
3 tablespoons dry sherry
1 tablespoon sugar
1 tablespoon cornstarch
½ teaspoon salt
1 large egg, beaten
⅓ cup water
½ cup all-purpose flour
1 pound skinned and boned chicken breast
    halves, cut into 1-inch pieces
¾ cup peanut oil
1 sweet red pepper, cut into strips
1 green pepper, cut into strips
1 small onion, sliced and separated into rings
Hot cooked rice

Drain pineapple, reserving juice; set pineapple
aside. Combine juice, vinegar, and next 5 ingredients, stirring until smooth; set aside.

Combine egg, water, and flour in a small
bowl; stir until blended. Add chicken to batter,
stirring until well coated.

Pour oil around top of preheated wok, coating
sides; heat at medium-high (350°) for 2 minutes.

Add half of chicken, and stir-fry until lightly
browned. Drain on paper towels; set aside.
Repeat with remaining chicken. Set aside.

Drain oil from wok, reserving 2 tablespoons in
wok; heat to 350°. Add red pepper, green pepper,
and onion; stir-fry 1 to 2 minutes or until crisp-
tender. Remove from wok; set aside.

Stir cornstarch mixture, and add to wok.
Cook, stirring constantly, until smooth and thickened. Add reserved chicken, vegetables, and
pineapple; stir gently, and cook until thoroughly
heated. Serve over rice. **Yield: 4 servings.**

Sizzling Walnut Chicken

4 skinned and boned chicken breast halves
1 tablespoon sherry
1 teaspoon salt
⅛ teaspoon pepper
2 egg whites
¼ cup cornstarch
2 to 2½ cups finely chopped walnuts
Vegetable oil
Gingered Plum Sauce

Cut chicken into bite-size pieces; sprinkle with sherry, salt, and pepper. Set aside.

Beat egg whites at high speed of an electric mixer until foamy. Gradually add cornstarch, beating until stiff peaks form. Gently fold in chicken. Roll each chicken piece in chopped walnuts.

Pour oil to depth of 2 inches into a large heavy skillet; heat to 350°. Fry chicken 5 to 6 minutes on each side or until golden brown. Drain on paper towels. Serve chicken with Gingered Plum Sauce. **Yield: 4 servings.**

Gingered Plum Sauce

1 cup plum jam
1 tablespoon ketchup
2 teaspoons grated lemon rind
1 tablespoon lemon juice
2 teaspoons cider vinegar
½ teaspoon ground ginger
½ teaspoon anise seeds, crushed
¼ teaspoon dry mustard
¼ teaspoon ground cinnamon
⅛ teaspoon ground cloves
⅛ teaspoon hot sauce

Heat plum jam in a small saucepan over medium heat until melted. Stir in remaining ingredients. Bring mixture to a boil; cook, stirring constantly, 1 minute. **Yield: 1¼ cups.**

Chicken Tempura Delight

1 large egg, beaten
2 tablespoons all-purpose flour
1 tablespoon water
½ teaspoon salt
2 pounds skinned and boned chicken breast halves, cut into 1-inch pieces
All-purpose flour
¾ cup peanut oil
Sweet-and-Sour Pineapple Sauce

Combine first 4 ingredients; mix well, and chill 1 hour. Dip chicken into batter; dredge in flour.

Pour oil around top of preheated wok, coating sides; heat at medium-high (350°) for 2 minutes. Add chicken, and stir-fry until lightly browned. Drain on paper towels. Serve with Sweet-and-Sour Pineapple Sauce. **Yield: 8 servings.**

Sweet-and-Sour Pineapple Sauce

1 (8-ounce) can crushed pineapple
1 (6-ounce) can unsweetened pineapple juice
2 tablespoons sugar
1 tablespoon cornstarch
2 teaspoons prepared mustard
2 tablespoons cider vinegar

Drain pineapple, reserving liquid. Combine reserved liquid and pineapple juice, adding enough water if necessary to equal 1 cup liquid. Combine ¾ cup juice and sugar in a small saucepan; cook over medium heat, stirring constantly, until sugar dissolves.

Combine cornstarch and remaining ¼ cup pineapple juice; stir into pineapple juice mixture in saucepan. Bring to a boil over medium heat, and boil 1 minute, stirring constantly.

Add mustard, vinegar, and pineapple; mix well. Chill. **Yield: 1½ cups.**

South by Southwest

From fajitas and flautas to tamales and chalupas, Southwestern chicken dishes offer a fiesta of tastes and colors. Now you can enjoy Mexico's unique flavors without leaving home.

Lime Soup, Spicy Tortilla Soup, No-Fuss Fajitas, Chicken Tamales

Spicy Tex-Mex Chicken, Chicken-Tomatillo Enchiladas, Pollo en Mole de Cacahuate

Chicken Flautas with Guacamole, Chicken-Olive Chalupas, Easy Chicken Enchiladas

Chicken Tostadas, Chilaquiles con Pollo, Mexican Chicken Rolls

Mexican Stir-Fry (page 124)

Lime Soup

1 (3- to 3½-pound) broiler-fryer, cut up
6 cups water
1 medium onion, quartered
1 stalk celery
3 fresh cilantro or parsley sprigs
6 whole peppercorns
2 teaspoons salt
½ teaspoon dried thyme
1 medium-size green pepper, chopped
1 medium onion, chopped
2 tablespoons vegetable oil
2 large tomatoes, peeled and chopped
1½ teaspoons grated lime rind
Juice of 2 limes
3 tablespoons chopped fresh cilantro or parsley
¼ teaspoon salt
¼ teaspoon pepper
8 corn tortillas
Vegetable oil
Garnishes: lime slices, fresh cilantro

Place first 8 ingredients in a large Dutch oven; bring to a boil. Cover, reduce heat, and simmer 1 hour. Remove chicken, reserving broth; let chicken cool. Bone and chop chicken; set aside. Strain broth to remove vegetables; set broth aside, and discard vegetables.

Cook green pepper and chopped onion in 2 tablespoons oil in Dutch oven, stirring constantly, until crisp-tender. Stir in tomato, and cook 5 minutes. Add reserved broth, lime rind, lime juice, and 3 tablespoons cilantro. Bring to a boil; reduce heat, and simmer, uncovered, 20 minutes.

Stir in chicken, ¼ teaspoon salt, and pepper; simmer, uncovered, 10 minutes.

Cut each tortilla into 8 wedges; fry in hot oil until crisp. Drain. To serve, place 8 tortilla wedges in each soup bowl; add soup, and garnish, if desired. **Yield: 2 quarts.**

Spicy Tortilla Soup

1 large onion, coarsely chopped
Vegetable oil
4 corn tortillas, coarsely chopped
6 cloves garlic, minced
1 tablespoon chopped fresh cilantro or parsley
2 (10¾-ounce) cans tomato puree
2 quarts chicken broth
1 tablespoon ground cumin
2 teaspoons chili powder
2 bay leaves
⅛ teaspoon ground red pepper
3 corn tortillas
2 skinned and boned chicken breast halves, cut into strips
1 avocado, peeled, seeded, and cubed
1 cup (4 ounces) shredded Cheddar cheese

Position knife blade in food processor bowl; add chopped onion, and process until smooth. Measure 1 cup onion puree, and set aside; reserve any remaining puree for another use.

Heat 3 tablespoons vegetable oil in a Dutch oven over medium heat; cook 4 chopped tortillas, garlic, and cilantro in hot oil until tortillas are soft.

Add 1 cup onion puree, tomato puree, and next 5 ingredients. Bring to a boil; cover, reduce heat, and simmer 30 minutes. Remove and discard bay leaves.

Cut 3 tortillas into thin strips. Pour oil to depth of ½ inch into a large, heavy skillet. Fry strips in hot oil over medium heat until browned. Remove tortillas, reserving ½ tablespoon oil in skillet; drain tortillas on paper towels, and set aside.

Add chicken strips to skillet; cook over medium heat, stirring constantly, about 8 minutes or until chicken is done.

Spoon soup into bowls; add chicken strips, avocado, and cheese. Top with tortilla strips. Serve immediately. **Yield: 2½ quarts.**

Spicy Tortilla Soup

No-Fuss Fajitas

No-Fuss Fajitas

3 tablespoons lemon juice
¾ teaspoon salt
¼ teaspoon coarsely ground pepper
¼ teaspoon garlic powder
½ teaspoon liquid smoke
3 skinned and boned chicken breast halves,
    cut into strips
6 (6-inch) flour tortillas
2 tablespoons vegetable oil
1 green or sweet red pepper, cut into strips
1 medium onion, sliced and separated into rings
Condiments: chopped tomato, green onions,
    lettuce, guacamole, sour cream, shredded
    cheese, and picante sauce

Combine first 5 ingredients in a medium bowl; reserve 1½ tablespoons marinade. Add chicken to remaining marinade in bowl; stir to coat. Cover and refrigerate at least 30 minutes. Drain chicken, discarding marinade.

Wrap tortillas in aluminum foil; bake at 350° for 15 minutes.

Heat oil in a heavy skillet. Add chicken; cook, stirring constantly, 2 to 3 minutes. Add 1½ tablespoons reserved marinade, pepper, and onion; cook, stirring constantly, until vegetables are crisp-tender. Remove from heat.

Divide mixture evenly, and spoon a portion onto each tortilla. If desired, top with several condiments; then wrap. **Yield: 6 fajitas.**

Flavors of Mexico

Cilantro or coriander: pungent herb that closely resembles flat leaf parsley
Jalapeño: hot green pepper (about 2 inches long); available fresh and canned
Tomatillo: small, firm green tomato-like fruit covered with a papery husk; tastes similar to a slightly green plum

Chicken Flautas with Guacamole

¼ cup chopped onion
1 clove garlic, minced
Vegetable oil
1½ teaspoons cornstarch
¼ cup chicken broth
1 cup cooked shredded chicken
½ teaspoon salt
¼ teaspoon pepper
2 tablespoons chopped green chiles
6 (6-inch) corn tortillas
Guacamole

Cook onion and garlic in 1 tablespoon oil in a skillet, stirring constantly, until tender; set aside.

Combine cornstarch and chicken broth; add cornstarch mixture, chicken, and next 3 ingredients to onion mixture. Cook over medium heat, stirring constantly, until mixture thickens; set aside.

Pour oil to depth of ¼ inch into a medium skillet; heat to 375°. Fry tortillas, one at a time, about 5 seconds on each side or just until softened. Drain on paper towels.

Spread about 2 tablespoons chicken mixture in center of each tortilla. Roll up each tortilla tightly, and secure with a wooden pick. Heat oil in skillet to 375°. Add flautas, and brown on all sides; drain on paper towels. Serve with Guacamole. **Yield: 2 servings.**

Guacamole

1 ripe avocado, peeled, seeded, and mashed
2 tablespoons chopped onion
1 medium tomato, peeled and chopped
1 clove garlic, minced
2 tablespoons lemon juice
¼ teaspoon salt
¼ teaspoon pepper

Combine all ingredients in a small bowl, stirring until blended. **Yield: 1¾ cups.**

Chicken Tamales

2 dozen dried cornhusks
2 (2½- to 3-pound) broiler-fryers, cut up
1 medium onion, chopped
1 tablespoon vegetable oil
1 (4-ounce) can taco sauce
1 teaspoon salt
1 teaspoon ground cumin
1 cup shortening
2 teaspoons chili powder
½ teaspoon salt
2½ cups instant corn masa
Commercial salsa

Cover dried cornhusks with hot water; let stand 1 hour or until softened. Drain well, and pat with paper towels to remove excess water.

Place chicken in a large Dutch oven; add water to cover. Bring to a boil over medium heat; cover, reduce heat, and simmer 45 minutes or until tender; drain, reserving 1 cup broth. Bone and finely chop chicken to make 4 cups. Set chopped chicken aside.

Cook onion in hot oil in a large skillet over medium heat until tender. Stir in chicken, taco sauce, 1 teaspoon salt, and cumin. Set aside.

Cream shortening; add reserved 1 cup broth, chili powder, and ½ teaspoon salt, mixing well. Gradually add corn masa, mixing well; beat 10 minutes at medium speed of a heavy-duty electric mixer until light and fluffy.

Cut each cornhusk to make a 4-inch square. Place about 2 tablespoons masa dough in center of each husk, spreading to within ½ inch of edges. Place about 2 tablespoons chicken mixture on dough, spreading evenly. Fold in one edge; roll up tamales, starting with an adjoining side, leaving opposite end open. Tie with string or narrow strip of softened cornhusk.

Place a steaming rack or metal colander in a large pot, and place a cup in center of rack. Add just enough water to fill pot below rack level to keep tamales above water. Stand tamales on folded ends around the cup. Bring water to a boil. Cover and steam 1 hour or until tamale dough pulls away from husks; add more water as necessary. Serve with salsa. **Yield: 2 dozen.**

Chicken-Olive Chalupas

Vegetable oil
6 (10-inch) flour tortillas
2 (16-ounce) cans refried beans
Chicken-Olive Filling
½ medium head iceberg lettuce, shredded
2 medium tomatoes, chopped
6 green onions, chopped
2 avocados, peeled and chopped
Taco sauce
Sour cream

Pour oil to depth of ¼ inch into a large skillet; heat to 375°.

Fry tortillas, one at a time, about 20 seconds on each side or until crisp and golden. Drain on paper towels.

Spread an equal amount of beans on each tortilla. Top with equal amounts of Chicken-Olive Filling and next 4 ingredients. Serve with taco sauce and sour cream. **Yield: 6 servings.**

Chicken-Olive Filling

2 (1.25-ounce) packages taco seasoning mix
2 cups water
3 cups chopped cooked chicken
1 (6-ounce) can pitted ripe olives, drained and sliced

Combine taco seasoning mix and water in a medium skillet, stirring well; bring to a boil. Reduce heat, and simmer 5 minutes, stirring occasionally.

Stir in chicken and olives; simmer 3 additional minutes. **Yield: about 4 cups.**

Chicken Tostadas

Chicken Tostadas

4 skinned and boned chicken breast halves, cut into ¼-inch-wide strips
¼ cup chopped onion
2 tablespoons butter or margarine, melted
1 (16-ounce) jar salsa
1 (1¼-ounce) package taco seasoning mix
1 (16-ounce) can refried beans
1 (4½-ounce) package tostada shells
2 cups shredded lettuce
1 cup (4 ounces) shredded Cheddar cheese
2 small tomatoes, chopped

Cook half each of chicken strips and onion in 1 tablespoon butter in a large skillet over medium-high heat 2 to 3 minutes, stirring often. Remove mixture, and set aside. Repeat procedure with remaining chicken, onion, and butter.

Return chicken mixture to skillet; add salsa and taco seasoning mix. Cook over low heat 10 minutes, stirring occasionally.

Heat refried beans in a small saucepan; set aside.

Place tostada shells on a baking sheet, slightly overlapping. Bake at 350° for 5 minutes. Spread about 2 tablespoons refried beans on each tostada; top evenly with chicken mixture, lettuce, cheese, and tomato. **Yield: 6 servings.**

Mexican Tostadas

Our recipe is a slight variation of the crisp-fried corn or flour tortilla native to Mexico. Both are piled with beef or chicken, lettuce, tomato, and cheese.

Easy Chicken Enchiladas

2 cups chopped cooked chicken
2 cups sour cream
1 (10¾-ounce) can cream of chicken soup
1½ cups (6 ounces) shredded Monterey Jack cheese
1½ cups (6 ounces) shredded longhorn cheese
1 (4.5-ounce) can chopped green chiles, drained
2 tablespoons chopped onion
⅛ teaspoon salt
¼ teaspoon pepper
10 (10-inch) flour tortillas
Vegetable oil
1 cup (4 ounces) shredded longhorn cheese

Combine first 9 ingredients; mix well. Fry tortillas, one at a time, in 2 tablespoons oil in a skillet 5 seconds on each side or until softened; add additional oil, if necessary. Drain.

Place a heaping ½ cup chicken mixture on each tortilla; roll up each tortilla, and place seam side down in a 13- x 9- x 2-inch baking dish.

Cover and bake at 350° for 20 minutes. Sprinkle with 1 cup longhorn cheese, and bake, uncovered, 5 additional minutes. **Yield: 5 servings.**

Chicken-Tomatillo Enchiladas

5 skinned chicken breast halves
2 (3-ounce) packages cream cheese, softened
⅓ cup half-and-half
¾ cup finely chopped onion
½ teaspoon salt
Tomatillo Sauce
12 (6-inch) corn tortillas
¾ cup (3 ounces) shredded Cheddar cheese
¾ cup (3 ounces) shredded Monterey Jack cheese
Condiments: shredded lettuce, chopped tomatoes, sliced ripe olives, sour cream

Place chicken in a Dutch oven; add water to cover. Bring to a boil; cover, reduce heat, and simmer 35 minutes or until tender.

Remove chicken, reserving 2½ cups broth for Tomatillo Sauce. Bone and chop chicken; set aside.

Beat cream cheese and half-and-half at medium speed of an electric mixer until smooth. Stir in chicken, onion, and salt; set aside.

Spread ¾ cup Tomatillo Sauce in a lightly greased 13-x 9- x 2-inch baking dish; set aside.

Soften tortillas according to package directions.

Spread about 1½ tablespoons Tomatillo Sauce over each tortilla; spoon ¼ cup chicken mixture down center of each. Roll up tortillas, and place, seam side down, in baking dish.

Cover and bake enchiladas at 350° for 25 minutes.

Sprinkle with cheeses. Serve with remaining Tomatillo Sauce and condiments. **Yield: 6 servings.**

Tomatillo Sauce

½ pound fresh tomatillos
4 to 6 jalapeño peppers, seeded and chopped
2½ cups reserved chicken broth
2 tablespoons cornstarch
2 tablespoons water
2 tablespoons chopped fresh cilantro or parsley
1 teaspoon salt

Remove husks from tomatillos; rinse tomatillos.

Combine tomatillos, peppers, and broth in a saucepan. Bring to a boil; reduce heat, and simmer 6 minutes.

Combine cornstarch and water; stir into tomatillo mixture. Add cilantro and salt. Bring to a boil; boil, stirring constantly, 1 minute. Cool slightly.

Pour into container of an electric blender or food processor; process until smooth, stopping once to scrape down sides. **Yield: 3 cups.**

Note: Two (11-ounce) cans tomatillos, drained and chopped, may be substituted for fresh tomatillos.

Chicken-Tomatillo Enchiladas

Chilaquiles con Pollo

1 (3- to 3½-pound) broiler-fryer
6 cups water
1 teaspoon salt
Vegetable oil
4 (8-ounce) packages frozen corn tortillas, thawed
2 (10¾-ounce) cans cream of mushroom soup
2 (10¾-ounce) cans cream of chicken soup
2 (10-ounce) cans tomatoes and green chiles, undrained
2 (16-ounce) cans stewed tomatoes, undrained
1 fresh serrano chile or jalapeño pepper, broiled, peeled, seeded, and chopped
4 medium onions, chopped
1 bunch green onions, chopped
1½ teaspoons garlic powder
1 teaspoon ground cumin
5 cups (20 ounces) shredded Cheddar cheese
3 cups (12 ounces) shredded Monterey Jack cheese

Combine first 3 ingredients in a Dutch oven; bring to a boil. Cover, reduce heat, and simmer 1 hour or until chicken is tender.

Remove chicken from broth; cool and cut into bite-size pieces. Strain broth, and set aside 1⅓ cups (reserve remaining broth for another use).

Pour oil to depth of ⅛ inch in a large skillet; heat to 375°. Using tongs, carefully arrange 3 tortillas in oil; cook 3 to 5 seconds on each side. Drain on paper towels. Repeat cooking procedure with remaining tortillas; add oil to skillet if necessary. Tear each tortilla into 8 pieces; set aside. Reserve oil in skillet.

Combine reserved 1⅓ cups broth, mushroom soup, and next 4 ingredients in Dutch oven; simmer 30 minutes, stirring frequently.

Cook onions, garlic powder, and cumin in reserved oil in skillet until onions are tender but not brown. Stir onions and chicken into soup mixture.

Spread one-fourth of tortillas in a 13- x 9- x 2-inch baking dish. Sprinkle half of Cheddar cheese over tortillas; pour one-fourth of sauce over cheese. Spread one-fourth of tortillas over sauce. Pour one-fourth of sauce over tortillas; sprinkle top with half of Monterey Jack cheese.

Repeat layering sequence in another 13- x 9- x 2-inch baking dish. Bake casseroles at 350° for 20 to 30 minutes or until bubbly. **Yield: 24 servings.**

Note: Casseroles may be frozen before baking; thaw completely in refrigerator, and bake as directed.

Montezuma Tortilla Pie

2 cups peeled chopped tomato
2 small cloves garlic
¼ teaspoon sugar
½ teaspoon salt
½ cup water
3 tablespoons peanut or safflower oil
⅓ cup chopped onion
2 (4.5-ounce) cans chopped green chiles, drained
24 corn tortillas
Vegetable oil
2 cups chopped cooked chicken
1½ cups sour cream
1¾ cups (7 ounces) shredded Cheddar cheese

Combine first 5 ingredients in container of an electric blender; process 1 minute or until smooth. Pour into a skillet; cook 8 minutes over medium heat, stirring often. Set sauce aside.

Heat peanut oil in a skillet; add onion, and cook until tender. Add chiles; cover, reduce heat, and simmer 4 minutes. Set aside.

Fry tortillas, one at a time, in 2 tablespoons hot oil (375°) about 5 seconds on each side or just until tortillas are softened. Add additional oil, if necessary. Drain on paper towels.

Place 8 tortillas in a lightly greased 13- x 9- x 2-inch baking dish. Layer half each of chicken and chile mixture; top with one-third each of sauce, sour cream, and cheese.

Repeat all layers, starting with tortillas; top with

remaining tortillas, sauce, sour cream, and cheese.

Bake at 350° for 25 minutes; serve immediately.
Yield: 6 to 8 servings.

Breast-of-Chicken Fiesta

1 cup Cheddar cheese cracker crumbs
2 tablespoons taco seasoning mix
8 skinned and boned chicken breast halves
4 green onions, chopped
2 tablespoons butter or margarine, melted
2 cups whipping cream
1 cup (4 ounces) shredded Monterey Jack cheese
1 cup (4 ounces) shredded Cheddar cheese
1 (4.5-ounce) can chopped green chiles, drained
½ teaspoon chicken-flavored bouillon granules

Combine cracker crumbs and seasoning mix
in a small bowl, stirring well. Dredge chicken in
crumb mixture; place in a greased 13- x 9- x 2-
inch baking dish.

Cook green onions in butter in a large skillet
over medium heat until tender. Stir in whipping
cream and remaining ingredients; pour over
chicken. Bake, uncovered, at 350° for 45 minutes.
Yield: 8 servings.

Start with Tortillas

<u>Chalupa:</u> fried tortilla spread with
an assortment of toppings
<u>Enchilada:</u> softened tortilla filled
with meat or cheese and rolled or
folded before being topped with a
sauce and baked
<u>Fajita:</u> originally made with mari-
nated, grilled skirt steak; also popular with chicken cut into strips
and wrapped in warm flour tortillas
<u>Flauta:</u> corn tortilla rolled around
chicken or meat and fried until crisp

Mexican Pollo en Pipián

6 dried ancho chiles
½ cup hot water
1 (4-pound) broiler-fryer, cut up
2 medium onions, quartered
½ green pepper, cut into strips
2 carrots, cut into 4 pieces
1 (10½-ounce) can chicken broth
3½ cups water
1 teaspoon dried coriander seeds
¼ cup creamy peanut butter
½ teaspoon salt
¼ teaspoon ground cinnamon
¼ teaspoon dried thyme
⅛ teaspoon ground cloves
Hot cooked rice
Flour tortillas

Remove stems and seeds from chiles. Chop
chiles; combine chiles and ½ cup hot water in a
small bowl; cover and set aside 1 hour. Drain
well, and set chiles aside.

Combine chicken and next 5 ingredients in a
large Dutch oven. Place coriander seeds on a 6-
inch square of cheesecloth; tie with string. Add
cheesecloth bag to chicken mixture. Bring to a
boil; cover, reduce heat, and simmer 1 hour.

Remove chicken and vegetables from broth;
set aside. Remove and discard cheesecloth bag.
Strain broth; reserve 1 cup broth, and return 2
cups remaining broth to Dutch oven. Let chicken
cool; skin, bone, and chop chicken; return chick-
en and vegetables to Dutch oven.

Combine chiles and reserved 1 cup chicken
broth in container of an electric blender; process
until smooth. Add peanut butter; process until
smooth. Add peanut butter mixture, salt, and next
3 ingredients to chicken mixture; stir well. Bring
to a boil; cover, reduce heat, and simmer 30 minutes.
Serve over rice with tortillas. **Yield: 4 servings.**

Mexican Chicken Rolls

½ cup fine, dry breadcrumbs
¼ cup grated Parmesan cheese
1 teaspoon chili powder
¼ teaspoon ground cumin
¼ teaspoon pepper
8 skinned and boned chicken breast halves
1 (8-ounce) package Monterey Jack cheese
 with peppers
⅓ cup butter or margarine, melted

Combine first 5 ingredients in a shallow dish; set aside.

Place chicken between 2 sheets of heavy-duty plastic wrap; flatten to ¼-inch thickness, using a meat mallet or rolling pin. Cut cheese crosswise into 8 equal slices; place a slice of cheese on each chicken breast. Roll up from short side, and secure with wooden picks.

Dip chicken rolls in butter, and dredge in breadcrumb mixture. Place rolls, seam side down, in a lightly greased 11- x 7- x 1½-inch baking dish; bake at 350° for 25 to 30 minutes. **Yield: 8 servings.**

Mexican Stir-Fry

(pictured on page 113)

4 skinned and boned chicken breast halves
2 tablespoons Mexican-seasoned chili powder
2 teaspoons cornstarch
½ cup chicken broth
2 tablespoons olive oil, divided
1 cup frozen whole kernel corn, thawed
2 medium tomatoes, seeded and diced
1 cup canned black beans, drained
¼ teaspoon salt

Cut chicken into thin strips; toss with chili powder, coating well. Let stand 10 minutes. Combine cornstarch and chicken broth; set aside.

Pour 1 tablespoon oil around top of preheated wok or skillet, coating sides; heat at medium-high (350°) for 2 minutes. Add chicken; stir-fry 3 to 4 minutes. Remove from wok, and set aside.

Pour remaining 1 tablespoon olive oil into wok; add corn and tomato, and stir-fry 2 minutes. Return reserved chicken to wok. Add broth mixture, beans, and salt; cook, stirring constantly, until thickened. **Yield: 4 servings.**

Spicy Tex-Mex Chicken

4 large eggs, beaten
¼ cup green chile salsa
¼ teaspoon salt
2 cups fine, dry breadcrumbs
2 teaspoons chili powder
2 teaspoons ground cumin
1½ teaspoons garlic salt
½ teaspoon ground oregano
6 skinned and boned chicken breast halves
¼ cup butter or margarine
Shredded lettuce
1 (8-ounce) carton sour cream
⅓ cup chopped green onions
12 cherry tomatoes
Garnishes: avocado slices, lime wedges
Additional salsa

Combine first 3 ingredients in a shallow bowl; set aside.

Combine breadcrumbs and next 4 ingredients in a shallow pan, and mix well.

Dip chicken in egg mixture, and dredge in breadcrumb mixture; repeat, and set aside.

Melt butter in a 13- x 9- x 2-inch pan. Place chicken in pan, turning once to coat with butter. Bake, uncovered, at 375° for 30 to 35 minutes.

Arrange chicken on a bed of shredded lettuce on a large platter. Top each serving with a dollop of sour cream, and sprinkle with green onions; arrange cherry tomatoes on platter. Garnish, if desired; serve with additional salsa. **Yield: 6 servings.**

Grilled Lime-Jalapeño Chicken

4 skinned and boned chicken breast halves
¼ cup vegetable oil
½ cup lime or lemon juice
1½ teaspoons garlic powder
1 tablespoon minced jalapeño pepper
¼ teaspoon salt
⅛ teaspoon pepper
Garnishes: lime wedges, jalapeño peppers,
   cherry tomatoes, fresh parsley sprigs

Place chicken between 2 sheets of heavy-duty plastic wrap; flatten to ¼-inch thickness, using a meat mallet or rolling pin. Set aside.

Combine oil and next 3 ingredients; reserve ¼ cup marinade and refrigerate. Place remaining marinade in a heavy-duty, zip-top plastic bag. Add chicken; seal and marinate in refrigerator 1 hour. Remove chicken from marinade, discarding marinade.

Sprinkle chicken with salt and pepper. Grill chicken, covered with grill lid, over medium-hot coals (350° to 400°) 7 minutes on each side, basting twice with reserved ¼ cup marinade. Garnish, if desired. **Yield: 4 servings.**

Grilled Lime-Jalapeño Chicken

Poached Chicken with Black Beans and Salsa

1 cup chicken broth
6 skinned and boned chicken breast halves
¼ cup dry white wine
¼ teaspoon salt
¼ teaspoon pepper
1 (15-ounce) can black beans, undrained
2 teaspoons balsamic or red wine vinegar
Dash of red pepper
Salsa

Bring chicken broth to a boil in a large skillet. Add chicken and next 3 ingredients; cover, reduce heat, and simmer 15 to 20 minutes. Remove from heat.

Pour beans into a container of an electric blender; process until smooth. Combine beans, vinegar, and red pepper in a saucepan; heat thoroughly, stirring occasionally. Add 1 to 2 tablespoons broth from chicken if mixture is too thick.

Divide bean mixture on individual serving plates; drain chicken, and arrange over bean puree. Top with salsa. Serve immediately. **Yield: 6 servings.**

Salsa

1 large tomato, diced
1 serrano or other hot green chile pepper, minced
1 small onion, diced
1 clove garlic, minced
½ cup cilantro or parsley, finely chopped
¼ teaspoon salt
⅛ teaspoon pepper

Combine all ingredients; refrigerate 2 to 3 hours. **Yield: 1½ cups.**

Pollo en Mole de Cacahuate (Chicken with Peanut Mole Sauce)

1 (3-pound) broiler-fryer, cut up and skinned
Salt
1 teaspoon paprika
All-purpose flour
1 cup vegetable oil
¼ cup all-purpose flour
3 tablespoons creamy peanut butter
2 cloves garlic, pressed
2 tablespoons chili powder
1 teaspoon ground cumin
2½ cups water
1 teaspoon Worcestershire sauce
¼ teaspoon salt
Garnish: fresh parsley sprigs

Season chicken with salt and paprika; dredge in flour. Brown chicken in hot oil over medium heat in a large skillet. Remove chicken from skillet, and drain on paper towels; reserve ⅓ cup pan drippings. Place chicken in a 13- x 9- x 2-inch baking dish.

Return reserved pan drippings to skillet; stir in ¼ cup flour, and cook, stirring constantly, 1 minute. Add peanut butter and next 3 ingredients; cook, stirring constantly, until bubbly. Gradually add water; cook over medium heat, stirring until thickened. Stir in Worcestershire sauce and ¼ teaspoon salt.

Pour sauce over chicken; bake, uncovered, at 350° for 30 minutes. Garnish, if desired. **Yield: 4 servings.**

Sauce It

<u>Mole:</u> highly seasoned sauce often served with chicken; may contain Mexican chocolate but not essential
<u>Salsa:</u> cooked or uncooked sauce made with tomatoes, chiles, and seasonings

Outdoor Specialties

Nothing from the grill tastes better than chicken. So fire up
the coals, sniff the enticing aroma, and savor
the tantalizing flavors of these winners.

Grilled Cumin Chicken, Grilled Teriyaki Chicken, Grilled Chicken

Garlic-Grilled Chicken, Basil-Grilled Chicken, Pesto Chicken with Basil Cream

Chicken with White Barbecue Sauce, Marinated Chicken Breasts, Chicken Kabobs

Soy-Lime Grilled Chicken Thighs, Grilled Ginger-Orange Chicken

Spicy Southwest Barbecue Sauce (page 140)

Grilled Cumin Chicken

2 (2½- to 3-pound) broiler-fryers, quartered
Juice of 3 lemons
2 tablespoons vegetable oil
2 tablespoons ground cumin
1 teaspoon salt
1 tablespoon coarsely ground pepper
2½ teaspoons celery salt
¼ teaspoon red pepper

Place chicken in a large shallow dish; pour lemon juice over chicken. Cover and marinate in refrigerator 2 to 3 hours, turning once. Remove chicken from lemon juice; rub with oil.

Combine cumin and remaining ingredients; stir well. Sprinkle seasoning over chicken.

Grill chicken, skin side up, over medium-hot coals (350° to 400°) 30 to 35 minutes or until done, turning once. **Yield: 8 servings.**

Chicken with White Barbecue Sauce

1½ cups mayonnaise
⅓ cup apple cider vinegar
¼ cup lemon juice
2 tablespoons sugar
2 tablespoons freshly ground pepper
2 tablespoons white wine Worcestershire sauce
1 (2½- to 3-pound) broiler-fryer, quartered

Combine first 6 ingredients in a small bowl; stir well. Arrange chicken in a shallow dish; pour ¾ cup sauce over chicken, turning to coat. Cover and refrigerate remaining sauce. Cover chicken and marinate in refrigerator 6 to 8 hours, turning occasionally.

Remove chicken, discarding marinade; arrange in a 12- x 8- x 2-inch baking dish with skin side down and thicker portion of chicken toward outside of dish. Cover with wax paper, and microwave at HIGH 10 to 12 minutes; turn and rearrange chicken after 5 minutes.

Grill chicken, skin side up, over medium-hot coals (350° to 400°) 15 to 20 minutes or until done, turning once and basting with half of reserved marinade. Serve with remaining reserved sauce. **Yield: 4 servings.**

Grilled Teriyaki Chicken

4 cups dry white wine
½ cup lemon juice
¼ cup teriyaki sauce
1 tablespoon minced onion
1 clove garlic, minced
2 bay leaves
1 tablespoon bouquet garni
½ teaspoon seasoned salt
½ teaspoon seasoned pepper
½ teaspoon lemon-pepper seasoning
2 black peppercorns
2 (2½- to 3-pound) broiler-fryers, halved
Garnishes: lemon slices, curly endive

Combine first 11 ingredients in a large shallow container; mix well. Reserve 2 cups marinade, and refrigerate. Place chicken in container; cover and marinate in refrigerator 8 hours, turning chicken often. Remove chicken and discard marinade.

Grill chicken, covered with grill lid, over medium-hot coals (350° to 400°) 50 to 60 minutes or until done, turning and basting often with reserved marinade. Garnish, if desired. **Yield: 4 to 8 servings.**

Microwave Speeds Grilling

Give chicken a jump-start by partially cooking it in the microwave and immediately finishing it on the grill. While coals are heating, microwave chicken at HIGH 3 to 5 minutes per pound; then grill 15 to 20 minutes.

Grilled Teriyaki Chicken

Soy-Lime Grilled Chicken Thighs

Soy-Lime Grilled Chicken Thighs

8 large chicken thighs, skinned (about 2 pounds)
½ cup soy sauce
¼ cup chopped green onions
¼ cup lime juice
2 tablespoons dark brown sugar
1 tablespoon honey
1 teaspoon crushed red pepper
1 large clove garlic, crushed
Garnishes: lime wedges, fresh parsley sprigs

Place chicken in an 11- x 7- x 1½-inch baking dish. Combine soy sauce and next 6 ingredients; stir well. Reserve ¼ cup marinade, and refrigerate. Pour remaining marinade over chicken. Cover and marinate in refrigerator 8 hours, turning occasionally.

Drain chicken, discarding marinade. Grill chicken, covered with grill lid, over medium-hot coals (350° to 400°) 8 minutes on each side or until done, basting frequently with reserved marinade. Garnish, if desired. **Yield: 4 servings.**

Soy-Lime Grilled Chicken Thighs Technique

Marinate these meaty chicken thighs in a mixture of soy sauce, lime juice, brown sugar, and seasonings.

Marinated Chicken Breasts

6 skinned and boned chicken breast halves
½ cup firmly packed brown sugar
⅓ cup olive oil
¼ cup cider vinegar
3 cloves garlic, crushed
3 tablespoons coarse-grain mustard
1½ tablespoons lemon juice
1½ tablespoons lime juice
1½ teaspoons salt
¼ teaspoon pepper

Place chicken in a large shallow dish. Combine remaining ingredients; stir well, and pour over chicken. Cover and marinate in refrigerator 2 hours.

Remove chicken from marinade, discarding marinade. Grill chicken, covered with grill lid, over medium-hot coals (350° to 400°) 8 to 10 minutes on each side or until done. **Yield: 6 servings.**

Grilled Chicken

½ cup white vinegar
½ cup balsamic vinegar
½ cup water
1 teaspoon chili powder
½ teaspoon dried oregano
½ teaspoon freshly ground black pepper
1 bay leaf, crushed
4 skinned and boned chicken breast halves

Combine first 7 ingredients; reserve ¼ cup marinade, and refrigerate. Place remaining marinade and chicken in a heavy-duty, zip-top plastic bag. Seal and marinate in refrigerator 20 minutes; remove chicken from marinade, discarding marinade.

Grill chicken, covered with grill lid, over medium-hot coals (350° to 400°) 8 to 10 minutes on each side, basting twice with reserved marinade. **Yield: 4 servings.**

From top: Grilled Ginger-Orange Chicken and Grilled Chicken with Vegetables Vinaigrette

Grilled Ginger-Orange Chicken

¼ cup orange marmalade
¼ cup Dijon mustard
2 tablespoons orange juice
2 green onions, finely chopped
6 skinned chicken breast halves
Ginger Butter
Garnishes: orange wedges, kale, green onion, orange rind strips

Combine first 4 ingredients; brush on both sides of chicken. Grill chicken, uncovered, over medium coals (300° to 350°) 9 to 10 minutes on each side or until done. Serve with Ginger Butter; garnish, if desired. **Yield: 6 servings.**

Ginger Butter

½ cup butter or margarine, softened
½ teaspoon grated orange rind
¼ teaspoon ground ginger

Combine all ingredients; chill. Shape butter into curls, if desired. **Yield: ½ cup.**

Grilled Chicken with Vegetables Vinaigrette

4 skinned and boned chicken breast halves
1 (16-ounce) bottle olive oil vinaigrette salad dressing, divided
2 sweet red peppers, seeded
2 small zucchini
2 carrots, scraped
2 small yellow squash

Combine chicken and ¾ cup salad dressing in a shallow dish; cover and marinate in refrigerator 4 hours.

Cut vegetables into ¼-inch strips; place in a shallow dish. Add ¾ cup salad dressing, tossing to coat. Cover and marinate in refrigerator 4 hours.

Remove chicken from marinade, discarding marinade. Grill chicken, covered with grill lid, over medium coals (300° to 350°) 5 to 6 minutes on each side, basting twice with remaining salad dressing.

Remove vegetables from marinade; drain and discard marinade. Arrange vegetables in steaming rack, and place over boiling water. Cover and steam 3 to 4 minutes or until crisp-tender. Serve chicken on steamed vegetables. **Yield: 4 servings.**

Garlic-Grilled Chicken

4 skinned and boned chicken breast halves
1 cup picante sauce
2 tablespoons vegetable oil
1 tablespoon lime juice
2 cloves garlic, minced
½ teaspoon ground cumin
½ teaspoon dried oregano, crushed
¼ teaspoon salt
Additional picante sauce

Place chicken between 2 pieces of heavy-duty plastic wrap; flatten to ¼-inch thickness, using a meat mallet or rolling pin. Cut chicken into 1-inch-wide strips; place in a shallow container.

Combine picante sauce and next 6 ingredients, mixing well. Reserve ⅓ cup marinade, and refrigerate. Pour remaining marinade over chicken; cover and marinate in refrigerator 1 to 2 hours.

Thread chicken onto skewers; grill over medium-hot coals (350° to 400°) 6 to 8 minutes or until done, turning occasionally and basting with reserved marinade. Serve with picante sauce. **Yield: 4 servings.**

Pesto Chicken with Basil Cream

8 skinned and boned chicken breast halves
8 (1-ounce) slices prosciutto or ham
½ cup Pesto
¼ cup olive oil
2 cloves garlic, minced
¼ teaspoon pepper
Basil Cream
Garnish: fresh basil

Place chicken between two sheets of heavy-duty plastic wrap; flatten to ¼-inch thickness, using a meat mallet or rolling pin.

Place 1 slice of prosciutto and 1 tablespoon Pesto in center of each piece of chicken. Roll up crosswise, and secure with a wooden pick. Place in a pan; cover and refrigerate 8 hours, if desired. Let stand at room temperature 30 minutes before grilling.

Combine olive oil, garlic, and pepper. Grill chicken, covered with grill lid, over medium coals (300° to 350°) 15 to 20 minutes or until done, turning and brushing occasionally with olive oil mixture. Serve with Basil Cream. Garnish, if desired. **Yield: 8 servings.**

Pesto

2 cups packed fresh basil
2 cloves garlic
¼ teaspoon salt
¼ teaspoon freshly ground pepper
½ cup freshly grated Parmesan cheese
½ cup freshly grated Romano cheese
½ cup olive oil

Remove stems from basil. Wash basil leaves thoroughly in lukewarm water, and drain well.

Position knife blade in food processor bowl. Add basil and next 5 ingredients, and top with cover; process until smooth. With food processor running, pour oil through food chute in a slow, steady stream until combined. **Yield: 1 cup.**

Basil Cream

⅓ cup dry white wine
3 shallots, chopped (about ¼ cup)
1½ cups whipping cream
¼ cup minced fresh basil
1 cup chopped tomato

Combine wine and shallots in a medium saucepan; bring to a boil, and cook about 2 minutes or until liquid is reduced to about ¼ cup.

Add whipping cream; return to a boil, and cook, stirring constantly, 8 to 10 minutes or until reduced to about 1 cup. Stir in basil and tomato; cook just until heated. **Yield: about 2 cups.**

Note: Chicken may be grilled in advance and reheated. To reheat, reserve ¼ cup basting mixture, and chill. Place chicken rolls on jellyroll pan; cover with foil, and chill. Remove from refrigerator; let stand at room temperature 30 minutes. Reheat chicken rolls, covered, at 350° for 15 to 20 minutes. Uncover and brush chicken with reserved basting mixture. Bake, uncovered, 5 to 10 additional minutes or until thoroughly heated.

Double-Up Grilling

• Grill extra chicken and enjoy it later served cold or reheated in the microwave.
• Leftover grilled chicken is delicious in salads and pasta dishes.
• Grilled chicken may be frozen up to 3 months. Defrost in refrigerator or at LOW (10% power) in the microwave.

Basil-Grilled Chicken

¾ teaspoon coarsely ground pepper
4 skinned chicken breast halves
⅓ cup butter or margarine, melted
¼ cup chopped fresh basil
½ cup butter or margarine, softened
2 tablespoons minced fresh basil
1 tablespoon grated Parmesan cheese
¼ teaspoon garlic powder
⅛ teaspoon salt
⅛ teaspoon pepper
Garnish: fresh basil sprigs

Press ¾ teaspoon pepper into meaty sides of chicken. Combine ⅓ cup melted butter and ¼ cup chopped basil; stir well. Set aside half of butter mixture. Brush chicken lightly with remaining butter mixture.

Combine ½ cup softened butter and next 5 ingredients in a small bowl; beat at low speed of an electric mixer until blended and smooth. Transfer to a small serving bowl; set aside.

Grill chicken over medium coals (300° to 350°) 8 to 10 minutes on each side, basting frequently with reserved melted butter mixture.

Serve chicken with basil-butter mixture. Garnish, if desired. **Yield: 4 servings.**

Basil-Grilled Chicken

Sesame Chicken Kabobs

6 skinned and boned chicken breast halves
¼ cup plus 2 tablespoons teriyaki sauce
¼ cup soy sauce
2 tablespoons sesame seeds
3 tablespoons vegetable oil
2 tablespoons dark sesame oil
2 medium-size sweet red peppers, cut into
     1-inch pieces
2 medium-size yellow peppers, cut into 1-inch
     pieces
4 small purple onions, cut into wedges
Garnish: fresh basil sprigs

   Cut chicken into 1-inch pieces; arrange in a
shallow container.
   Combine teriyaki sauce and next 4 ingredients, stirring well. Reserve ⅓ cup marinade, and
refrigerate. Pour remaining marinade over chick-
en; cover and marinate in refrigerator 3 hours.
   Soak 6 (12-inch) wooden skewers in water at
least 30 minutes. Remove chicken from marinade, discarding marinade. Thread chicken alter-
nately with peppers and onion onto skewers.
   Grill kabobs, covered with grill lid, over medium-hot coals (350° to 400°) 3 to 5 minutes on
each side or until chicken is done, basting frequently with reserved marinade. Garnish, if
desired. **Yield: 6 servings.**

Mastering Marinades

• Because chicken absorbs flavors
quickly, it doesn't necessarily require
lengthy marinating time.
• Marinate chicken in the refrigerator in a glass or non-metallic bowl
or a heavy-duty, zip-top plastic bag.
• Drain chicken and discard marinade.
To baste chicken during grilling, use a
portion of marinade previously set aside.

Sesame Chicken Kabobs Techniques

Seed peppers by cutting them in half and removing seeds and membranes with hands.

Chicken pieces quickly absorb the strong flavor combination of dark sesame oil, teriyaki sauce, and soy sauce.

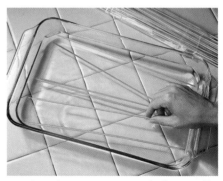

Soak wooden skewers in water before grilling. This prevents them from burning on the grill.

Sesame Chicken Kabobs

Chicken Kabobs

8 slices bacon, cut in half
4 skinned and boned chicken breast halves
1 (15¼-ounce) can unsweetened pineapple
    chunks
1 large onion, cut into 16 pieces
2 large green peppers, cut into 16 pieces
16 cherry tomatoes
½ cup white wine
3 tablespoons Worcestershire sauce
⅛ teaspoon pepper

Cook bacon in a skillet 1 to 3 minutes or until transparent; drain and set aside.

Cut each chicken breast into 4 strips. Drain pineapple, reserving juice. Combine chicken, pineapple chunks, bacon, onion, green pepper, and cherry tomatoes in a shallow dish.

Combine ½ cup reserved pineapple juice, wine, and remaining ingredients; stir well. Reserve ⅓ cup marinade, and refrigerate. Pour remaining marinade over chicken mixture; cover and marinate in refrigerator 8 hours, stirring occasionally.

Drain and discard marinade. Wrap a piece of bacon around each piece of chicken; alternate with vegetables on skewers.

Grill kabobs about 6 inches from medium-hot coals (350° to 400°) 20 minutes or until done, turning and basting often with reserved marinade. **Yield: 4 servings.**

Chicken Kabobs Supreme

4 skinned and boned chicken breast halves
½ cup vegetable oil
¼ cup soy sauce
¼ cup Chablis or other dry white wine
¼ cup light corn syrup
1 tablespoon sesame seeds
2 tablespoons lemon juice
¼ teaspoon garlic powder
¼ teaspoon ground ginger
1 small pineapple, cut into 1-inch pieces
1 large green pepper, cut into 1-inch pieces
2 medium onions, quartered
3 small zucchini, cut into 1-inch pieces
½ pound fresh mushroom caps
1 pint cherry tomatoes (optional)

Cut chicken into 1-inch pieces; arrange in a shallow dish, and set aside.

Combine oil and next 7 ingredients; mix well. Reserve ½ cup marinade, and refrigerate. Pour remaining marinade over chicken; cover and marinate in refrigerator at least 2 hours.

Remove chicken from marinade, discarding marinade. Alternate chicken, pineapple, and vegetables on skewers.

Grill kabobs about 6 inches from medium-hot coals (350° to 400°) 15 to 20 minutes or until done, turning and basting often with reserved marinade. **Yield: 6 servings.**

Hot Tips for Grilling

- **Leave** the skin on when grilling and remove it before eating, if desired, to prevent dryness.
- **Flatten** chicken halves with heel of hand before placing on grill for even cooking.
- **Handle** chicken with tongs instead of a fork to prevent piercing and loss of juices.
- **Cook** chicken until well done, not medium or rare. An instant-read thermometer should reach a temperature of 180° or, for boneless parts, an internal temperature of 160°.

Chicken Bundles
with Bacon Ribbons

12 whole skinned and boned chicken breasts
1 cup molasses
½ teaspoon ground ginger
¼ teaspoon garlic powder
2 tablespoons Worcestershire sauce
¼ cup soy sauce
¼ cup olive oil
¼ cup lemon juice
2 pounds mushrooms, sliced and divided
20 green onions, sliced and divided
½ cup butter, melted and divided
½ to 1 teaspoon spike seasoning, divided
24 slices bacon

Place chicken between two sheets of heavy-duty plastic wrap; flatten to ¼-inch thickness, using a meat mallet or rolling pin. Place chicken in a large shallow container, and set aside.

Combine molasses and next 6 ingredients; stir well. Reserve ½ cup marinade, and refrigerate. Pour remaining marinade over chicken, and marinate in refrigerator 8 hours.

Cook half each of mushrooms and green onions in ¼ cup butter, stirring constantly until liquid evaporates; add half of spike seasoning and stir well. Repeat process with remaining mushrooms, green onions, butter, and spike seasoning.

Make each chicken bundle by laying 2 slices bacon in a crosswise pattern on a flat surface. Place a whole chicken breast in center of bacon. Top each with 3 tablespoons mushroom mixture. Fold over sides and ends of chicken to make a square-shaped pouch. Pull bacon around, and tie ends under securely.

Grill chicken over low coals (under 300°) 45 to 55 minutes or until done, turning and basting with reserved marinade every 15 minutes. **Yield: 12 servings.**

Note: Spike seasoning can be found in most supermarkets.

Great Grilling

The key to perfectly grilled chicken is low temperature and non-rushed cooking time. When preparing the grill, consider whether you'll cook using direct or indirect heat.

Grilling with direct heat:
• **Arrange** the coals in a single layer; allow 1 pound charcoal to 2 pounds chicken. Light charcoal 30 minutes before grilling. If using a gas grill, preheat grill for 20 minutes. Coals are ready when covered with light gray ash.
• **Coat** food rack with cooking spray or vegetable oil; place rack 6 to 8 inches above coals.
• **Place** chicken on rack, skin side up, with smaller pieces near the edges.
• **Turn** chicken often during cooking for even doneness.

Grilling with indirect heat:
• **Place** 2 cups hickory or mesquite chips in center of a large square of aluminum foil; fold into a rectangle, and seal. Punch several holes in top of packet.
• **Arrange** charcoal or lava rocks on each side of grill, leaving center empty. Place packet on one side of coals or rocks, and ignite. Let charcoal burn 30 minutes until coals turn white. If using a gas grill, preheat grill for 20 minutes. Place a drip pan in center.
• **Coat** food rack with cooking spray or vegetable oil; place rack 6 to 8 inches above coals.
• **Place** chicken, skin side up, on rack directly over medium-hot coals (350° to 400°); cook, covered with grill lid, about 15 minutes.
• **Turn** chicken, and cook, covered with grill lid, 10 to 15 minutes or until golden. Move chicken over drip pan; cook, covered with grill lid, indirectly 25 to 35 minutes, brushing often with sauce and turning skin side up after 5 minutes.

Maple Syrup Barbecue Sauce

1 cup maple syrup
1 cup ketchup
1 cup finely chopped onion
¼ cup firmly packed brown sugar
¼ cup apple cider vinegar
¼ cup lemon juice
¼ cup water
2 tablespoons olive oil
2 tablespoons Worcestershire sauce
2 teaspoons finely chopped garlic
2 teaspoons grated lemon rind
1 teaspoon salt
¼ teaspoon hot sauce

Combine all ingredients in a saucepan.

Bring to a boil; reduce heat, and simmer 20 minutes. Cool.

Pour mixture into container of an electric blender; process until smooth.

Remove 1 cup sauce, and brush over chicken the last 30 minutes of cooking time. Serve chicken with remaining sauce. Refrigerate sauce up to 1 month. **Yield: 3½ cups.**

Herbed Lemon Barbecue Sauce

¾ cup lemon juice
2 cloves garlic, peeled
1 tablespoon onion powder
1½ teaspoons salt
1½ teaspoons paprika
1½ cups vegetable oil
1 tablespoon dried basil
1 teaspoon dried thyme

Combine first 5 ingredients in container of an electric blender; process on high 1 minute. With blender on high, add oil in a slow, steady stream; process 1 minute. Add basil and thyme; process on low 30 seconds.

Remove 1 cup sauce, and refrigerate.

Pour remaining sauce over chicken; cover and marinate in refrigerator 8 hours. Drain and blot off excess sauce.

Brush reserved 1 cup sauce over chicken the last 30 minutes of cooking time. **Yield: 2 cups.**

Spicy Southwest Barbecue Sauce

(pictured on page 127)

6 cloves garlic, unpeeled
2 cups ketchup
2 stalks celery, chopped
1 cup water
½ cup chopped onion
½ cup firmly packed brown sugar
½ cup butter or margarine
½ cup Worcestershire sauce
½ cup cider vinegar
3 tablespoons chili powder
2 teaspoons instant coffee granules
1½ to 2 teaspoons dried crushed red pepper
½ teaspoon salt
½ teaspoon ground cloves

Bake garlic in a small pan at 350° for 20 to 30 minutes or until lightly browned. Cool and peel.

Combine garlic and remaining ingredients in a medium saucepan.

Bring to a boil; reduce heat, and simmer 20 minutes. Cool.

Pour mixture into container of an electric blender; process until smooth, stopping once to scrape down sides.

Remove 1 cup sauce, and brush over chicken the last 30 minutes of cooking time. Serve chicken with remaining sauce. Refrigerate sauce up to 1 month. **Yield: 4½ cups.**

Easy Barbecue Sauce

Easy Barbecue Sauce

1 (16-ounce) can tomato sauce
1 cup chopped onion
½ cup Worcestershire sauce
¼ cup butter or margarine
¼ cup vegetable oil
2 tablespoons sugar
2 tablespoons dark brown sugar
2 teaspoons instant coffee granules
1 teaspoon salt
1 teaspoon garlic powder
1 teaspoon pepper
½ teaspoon ground ginger
½ teaspoon ground allspice

Combine all ingredients in a medium saucepan. Bring to a boil; reduce heat, and simmer 10 minutes, stirring occasionally.

Brush on chicken during grilling, broiling, or baking. Refrigerate sauce in a tightly covered container up to 1 month. **Yield: 3½ cups.**

Baste on a Sauce

Brush barbecue sauces onto chicken during the last 10 to 20 minutes of grilling, especially sauces that are tomato-based or contain sugar. These can cause flare-ups when basted on chicken directly over heat source.

Index

À la King, Chicken, 52
Appetizers
 Balls, Coconut Curried Chicken, 12
 Cheesecake, Chicken-Chile, 13
 Cheesecake, Curried Chicken, 15
 Cheesy Chicken-Tortilla Stack, 19
 Crêpes, Chicken, 22
 Dip, Tomato-Garlic, 16
 Drummettes, Southwestern Chicken, 16
 Fingers, Chicken Almondette, 18
 Nachos, Chicken, 19
 Pâté, Chicken Liver, 13
 Pâté, Wine, 13
 Pita, Peppery Chicken in, 21
 Pizza Crusts, Crispy, 18
 Pizza, Gruyère-Chicken, 18
 Rumaki, 15
 Sandwiches, Open-Faced Chicken, 22
 Sandwich, Marinated Chicken in a, 21
 Sauce, Curried Sour Cream, 15
 Sauce, Honey-Poppy Seed, 18
 Sauce, Mustard, 21
 Spread, Chicken Salad, 12
 Spread, Festive Chicken, 12
 Strips, Spicy Chicken, 16
 Wings, Hot Buffalo, 16
Asparagus-Chicken Salad, 30
Aspic-Topped Chicken Salad, 24

Bacon
 Ribbons, Chicken Bundles with Bacon, 139
 Salad, BLT Chicken, 33
Baked Chicken
 Almond Chicken, Spicy, 59
 Basil Chicken, 65
 Breast-of-Chicken Fiesta, 123
 Breasts Lombardy, Chicken, 75
 Cordon Bleu, Chicken, 76
 Country Captain Chicken, 91
 Creole Chicken, 57
 Dijon Chicken with Pasta, 71
 en Mole de Cacahuate Pollo (Chicken with Peanut Mole Sauce), 126
 en Papillote, Chicken and Vegetables, 84
 Foil, Chicken in, 59
 Fontina-Baked Chicken, 75
 Fruited Chicken, Golden, 65
 Herb Garden Chicken, 55
 Legs and Thighs, Barbecued Chicken, 60
 Lemon Chicken, Baked, 65
 Parmesan Chicken, 66
 Pecan Chicken, 66
 Rolls, Hearts of Palm Chicken, 78
 Rolls, Mexican Chicken, 124
 Rolls, Pesto-Stuffed Chicken, 78
 Roquefort Chicken, 76
 Rosemary-Riesling Chicken, 62
 Seasoned Chicken, Crunchy, 66
 Tarragon Chicken, 71
 Tex-Mex Chicken, Spicy, 124
 Walnut Chicken, Crispy, 60
Barbecued Chicken. *See also* Grilled Chicken, Sauces.
 Legs and Thighs, Barbecued Chicken, 60

 Oven-Barbecued Chicken, 60
 White Barbecue Sauce, Chicken with, 128
Basic Chicken Cookery, 9
Beans and Salsa, Poached Chicken with Black, 126
Boning a chicken breast, 10
Broccoli
 Divan Casserole, Chicken, 87
 Salad, Broccoli-Chicken, 30
 Soup, Creamy Chicken-and-Broccoli, 40
Brunswick Stew, 43
Butter, Ginger, 133
Butter Sauce, Green Peppercorn, 69
Buying and storing chicken, 7

Cacciatore, Chicken, 94
Casseroles
 Chilaquiles Con Pollo, 122
 Divan Casserole, Chicken, 87
 Enchiladas, Chicken-Tomatillo, 120
 Enchiladas, Easy Chicken, 120
 Lasagna, Chicken, 98
 Manicotti, Chicken, 97
 Salad Casserole, Hot Chicken, 36
 Shrimp-and-Chicken Casserole, 88
 Wild Rice Casserole, Chicken-, 91
Chalupas, Chicken-Olive, 118
Cheese
 Alouette, Chicken, 80
 Cheddar Dumplings, Chicken Ragout with, 52
 Chile Cheesecake, Chicken-, 13
 Curried Chicken Cheesecake, 15
 Fontina-Baked Chicken, 75
 Grits, Garlic-Cheese, 89
 Nachos, Chicken, 19
 Parmesan Chicken, 66
 Pesto, 134
 Pizza, Gruyère-Chicken, 18
 Roquefort Chicken, 76
 Roquefort Sauce, 76
 Spaghetti, Cheesy Chicken, 98
 Tart Shells, Cheese, 29
 Thighs, Fried Cheese-Stuffed Chicken, 103
 Tortilla Stack, Cheesy Chicken-, 19
Chilaquiles con Pollo, 122
Chili-Chicken Stew, 43
Chili, White Lightning Texas, 44
Cooking Techniques
 BLT Chicken Salad, 33
 Brunswick Stew, 43
 Cashew-Chicken Stir-Fry, 106
 Chicken in Mushroom Sauce, 73
 Chicken Salad in Puff Pastry, 26
 Double-Crust Chicken Pot Pie, 48
 Frying chicken, 9
 Golden Fruited Chicken, 65
 Grilling chicken, 9
 Mexican Chicken Salads, Hot, 36
 Microwaving chicken, 9
 Roasting chicken, 9
 Sesame Chicken Kabobs, 136
 Simmering chicken, 9
 Soy-Lime Grilled Chicken Thighs, 131
 Spinach-Stuffed Chicken in Puff Pastry, 83

Cordon Bleu, Chicken, 76
Crêpes, Basic, 22
Crêpes, Chicken, 22
Croquettes, Crispy Chicken, 104
Cuts of chicken, 6

D oneness tests for chicken, 8
Dressing, Tipsy Chicken and, 88
Drummettes, Orange-Pecan Chicken, 62
Drummettes, Southwestern Chicken, 16
Dumplings, Chicken Ragout with Cheddar, 52
Dumplings, Country Chicken and, 51

E nchiladas, Chicken-Tomatillo, 120
Enchiladas, Easy Chicken, 120

F ajitas, No-Fuss, 117
Filling, Chicken-Olive, 118
Flattening a chicken breast, 10
Flautas with Guacamole, Chicken, 117
Freezing and thawing guide, 8
Fried Chicken
    Crispy Fried Chicken, 101
    Croquettes, Crispy Chicken, 104
    Fingers, Chicken Almondette, 18
    Italian-Seasoned Fried Chicken, 101
    Kiev, Chicken, 104
    Spicy Fried Chicken, 101
    Strips, Spicy Chicken, 16
    Thighs, Fried Cheese-Stuffed Chicken, 103
    Walnut Chicken, Sizzling, 112
    Wings, Hot Buffalo, 16

G rilled Chicken. *See also* Barbecued Chicken.
    Basil Chicken, 65
    Basil-Grilled Chicken, 135
    Bundles with Bacon Ribbons, Chicken, 139
    Cumin Chicken, Grilled, 128
    Garlic-Grilled Chicken, 133
    Ginger-Orange Chicken, Grilled, 133
    Grilled Chicken, 131
    Kabobs, Chicken, 138
    Kabobs, Sesame Chicken, 136
    Kabobs Supreme, Chicken, 138
    Lime-Jalapeño Chicken, Grilled, 125
    Marinated Chicken Breasts, 131
    Pesto Chicken with Basil Cream, 134
    Salad, Grilled Chicken, 38
    Sandwich, Marinated Chicken in a, 21
    Teriyaki Chicken, Grilled, 128
    Thighs, Soy-Lime Grilled Chicken, 131
    Vegetables Vinaigrette, Grilled Chicken with, 133
Grits, Creole Chicken and, 89
Grits, Garlic-Cheese, 89
Guacamole, Chicken Flautas with, 117
Gumbo, Chicken-and-Oyster, 46
Gumbo, Chicken-and-Sausage, 44

K abobs
    Chicken Kabobs, 138
    Sesame Chicken Kabobs, 136
    Supreme, Chicken Kabobs, 138
Kiev, Chicken, 104

L asagna, Chicken, 98
Livers
    Pâté, Chicken Liver, 13
    Pâté, Wine, 13

Rumaki, 15
Sautéed Chicken Livers, 103

M anicotti, Chicken, 97
Marinated Chicken Breasts, 131
Marinating chicken, 10
Microwave
    Ginger-Nut Chicken, 92
    Mushroom Sauce, Chicken in, 73
    Pita, Peppery Chicken in, 21
    Rumaki, 15
    Stuffed Chicken, Wild Rice-, 56
    White Barbecue Sauce, Chicken with, 128

N oodle Soup, Chicken, 40
Nut Chicken, Ginger-, 92

P eppers
    Cheesecake, Chicken-Chile, 13
    Grilled Lime-Jalapeño Chicken, 125
    Topping, Rainbow Pepper, 68
Pesto, 134
Pesto Chicken with Basil Cream, 134
Pesto-Stuffed Chicken Rolls, 78
Piccata, Chicken, 102
Pies and Pastries
    Alouette, Chicken, 80
    Basic Pastry, 50
    Biscuit-Topped Chicken Pie, 51
    Biscuit Topping, 51
    Celery Seed Pastry, 48
    Chicken Salad in Puff Pastry, 26
    Ham Medley, Creamy Chicken-and-, 87
    Phyllo Pastry, Chicken Breasts in, 84
    Pot Pie, Double-Crust Chicken, 48
    Pot Pies, Individual Chicken, 50
    Puff Pastry Ring, 26
    Spinach-Stuffed Chicken in Puff Pastry, 83
    Tart Shells, Cheese, 29
    Tortilla Pie, Montezuma, 122
Pineapple
    Glaze, Roast Chicken with Pineapple-Mustard, 59
    Sauce, Sweet-and-Sour Pineapple, 112
Pizza Crusts, Crispy, 18
Pizza, Gruyère-Chicken, 18
Preparation Techniques
    Boning a chicken breast, 10
    Cutting chicken into strips, 10
    Flattening a chicken breast, 10
    Marinating chicken, 10
    Skinning chicken pieces, 10

Q uick chopped cooked chicken, 8
Quick Chicken, 68

R agout with Cheddar Dumplings, Chicken, 52
Rice
    Casserole, Chicken-Wild Rice, 91
    Pilaf, Chicken, 89
    Salad, Artichoke-Chicken-Rice, 30
    Soup, Chicken-and-Rice, 40
    Stuffed Chicken, Wild Rice-, 56
    Stuffed Roasted Chicken, Rice-, 56
Roasted Chicken
    Herb-Roasted Chicken, 55
    Pineapple-Mustard Glaze, Roast Chicken with, 59
    Rice-Stuffed Roasted Chicken, 56
Rosemary-Riesling Chicken, 62
Rumaki, 15

Salad Dressings
    Creamy Dressing, 33
    Italian Cream Dressing, 30
Salads
    Artichoke-Chicken-Rice Salad, 30
    Asparagus-Chicken Salad, 30
    Aspic-Topped Chicken Salad, 24
    BLT Chicken Salad, 33
    Broccoli-Chicken Salad, 30
    Chutney-Chicken Salad, 24
    Dilled Chicken Salad, 25
    Fruited Chicken Salad, 29
    Fruit Salad, Chicken-, 29
    Grilled Chicken Salad, 38
    Hot Chicken Salad Casserole, 36
    Hot Mexican Chicken Salads, 36
    Layered Chicken Salad, 33
    Marinated Chicken-Grape Salad, 29
    Old-Fashioned Chicken Salad, 24
    Oriental, Chicken Salad, 31
    Puff Pastry, Chicken Salad in, 26
    Rémoulade, Poulet, 25
    Southwestern Chicken Salad, 38
    Spread, Chicken Salad, 12
    Tortellini Salad, Chicken, 34
    Warm Chinese Chicken Salad, 34
Sandwiches
    Marinated Chicken in a Sandwich, 21
    Open-Faced Chicken Sandwiches, 22
    Pita, Peppery Chicken in, 21
Sauces
    Barbecue Sauce, Chicken with White, 128
    Barbecue Sauce, Easy, 141
    Barbecue Sauce, Herbed Lemon, 140
    Barbecue Sauce, Maple Syrup, 140
    Barbecue Sauce, Spicy Southwest, 140
    Basil and Cream Sauce, 68
    Basil Cream, 134
    Béarnaise Sauce, 78
    Chervil-and-Savory Sauce, 68
    Curried Sour Cream Sauce, 15
    Curry Sauce, Chicken, 69
    Green Peppercorn Butter Sauce, 69
    Ham Sauce, Country, 69
    Honey-Poppy Seed Sauce, 18
    Lemon Sauce, Chicken Scaloppine with, 102
    Mushroom Sauce, Chicken in, 73
    Mustard Sauce, 21
    Peanut Mole Sauce), Pollo en Mole de Cacahuate (Chicken with, 126
    Peppery Cream Sauce, 104
    Plum Sauce, Gingered, 112
    Red Hot Sauce, 62
    Roquefort Sauce, 76
    Salsa, 126
    Sweet-and-Sour Pineapple Sauce, 112
    Tomatillo Sauce, 120
Skinning chicken pieces, 10
Soups. See also Chili, Gumbo, Stews.
    Broccoli Soup, Creamy Chicken-and-, 40
    Lime Soup, 114
    Noodle Soup, Chicken, 40
    Rice Soup, Chicken-and-, 40
    Tortilla Soup, Spicy, 114
Spaghetti
    Cacciatore, Chicken, 94
    Cheesy Chicken Spaghetti, 98
    Tetrazzini, Creamy Chicken, 97
Spicy Almond Chicken, 59
Spicy Fried Chicken, 101
Spicy Tex-Mex Chicken, 124
Spinach-Stuffed Chicken in Puff Pastry, 83
Spread, Chicken Salad, 12
Spread, Festive Chicken, 12

Stews. See also Chili, Gumbo, Soups.
    Brunswick Stew, 43
    Burgoo, Kentucky, 46
    Chili-Chicken Stew, 43
Stir-Fried Chicken
    Cashew-Chicken Stir-Fry, 106
    Chinese, Chicken, 110
    Garden, Chicken-in-a-, 111
    Lemon Chicken and Vegetables, 109
    Mexican Stir-Fry, 124
    Orange Chicken Stir-Fry, 109
    Princess Chicken, 108
    Sweet-and-Sour Chicken, 111
    Szechuan Chicken with Cashews, 108
    Tempura Delight, Chicken, 112
    Vegetable Stir-Fry, Chicken-, 109
Storing chicken, buying and, 7
Stovetop Chicken
    à la King, Chicken, 52
    Almond Chicken, Creamy, 70
    Balls, Coconut Curried Chicken, 12
    Bourbon Chicken with Gravy, 103
    Champagne Chicken, 70
    Country Chicken and Dumplings, 51
    Creole Chicken and Grits, 89
    Curry, Chicken, 92
    Cutlets, Italian Chicken, 102
    Dijon-Herb Chicken, 71
    Fajitas, No-Fuss, 117
    Fettuccine Supreme, Chicken, 94
    Livers, Sautéed Chicken 103
    Mexican Pollo en Pipián, 123
    Piccata, Chicken, 102
    Pita, Peppery Chicken in, 21
    Poached Chicken with Black Beans and Salsa, 126
    Quick Chicken, 68
    Rollups, Chicken, 80
    Scaloppine with Lemon Sauce, Chicken, 102
    Tamales, Chicken, 118
    Tostadas, Chicken, 119
    Véronique, Chicken, 70

Tamales, Chicken, 118
Tarragon Chicken, 71
Techniques, Preparation, 10
Tempura Delight, Chicken, 112
Tetrazzini, Creamy Chicken, 97
Thawing guide, freezing and, 8
Thighs, Soy-Lime Grilled Chicken, 131
Tomatillo Enchiladas, Chicken-, 120
Tomatillo Sauce, 120
Tomatoes
    Dip, Tomato-Garlic, 16
    Salad, BLT Chicken, 33
Toppings
    Biscuit Topping, 51
    Guacamole, 117
    Pepper Topping, Rainbow, 68
Tortillas
    Cheesy Chicken-Tortilla Stack, 19
    Pie, Montezuma Tortilla, 122
    Soup, Spicy Tortilla, 114
Tostadas, Chicken, 119

Vegetables. See also Peppers, Tomatoes.
    en Papillote, Chicken and Vegetables, 84
    Foil, Chicken in, 59
    Garden Chicken, Herb, 55
    Garden, Chicken-in-a-, 111
    Grilled Chicken with Vegetables Vinaigrette, 133
    Lemon Chicken and Vegetables, 109
    Stir-Fry, Chicken-Vegetable, 109